Don't Let Them Drown

Officers' Children in the Storm of Appointment Change

Major Thomas McWilliams

Contributing Author
Brittany McWilliams

The Scripture passages used in this book are from the following translations:

Common English Bible (CEB)
Contemporary English Version (CEV)
English Standard Version (ESV)
New American Standard Bible (NASB)
New International Version (NIV)
New Revised Standard Version (NRSV)

Sources for quoted and referenced material are listed by page number in a Notes section at the back of the book.

For information, write:
The Salvation Army
USA Southern Territory
Literary Council
1424 Northeast Expressway
Atlanta GA 30329

ISBN: 978-0-86544-076-0

Cover Artwork: Erin Wyatt

Editors: Linda & Lynell Johnson, The WordWorking Shop

Printed in the United States of America

To a Lord who saved me,
A mother who nurtured me,
A wife who rescued me,
A daughter who inspired me.
Thank you!

Acknowledgments

I would not have been able to complete this book without the wonderful support of many godly individuals who have touched my life. This includes the young families of the AOK Division, who motivated me to produce this book as an aid to navigation for their families throughout their ministry life.

I'm forever thankful to The Salvation Army, especially Colonel John Needham and Major Barbara Getz, for supporting my work and allowing me to research and discuss this very important issue with the officers of the Southern Territory.

I'm especially indebted to the active, retired, and former officers of the Southern Territory who spoke into this work with great clarity and emotion through their anonymous responses to the officers' "felt needs" survey. This book is virtually a pulling together of their thoughts and feelings.

Finally, I thank the Lord for my beautiful wife of 25 years, Stacie, who has supported me fully in my ministry, and our fantastic daughter, Brittany, who has served as my inspiration to help other officer families.

If I had a child to raise over again,
I'd finger paint more, and point the fingers less.

I'd do less correcting, and more connecting.

I'd take my eyes off my watch, and watch with my eyes.

I would care to know less, and know to care more.

I'd take more hikes and fly more kites.

I'd stop playing serious, and seriously play.

I would run through more fields, and gaze at more stars.

I'd do more hugging, and less tugging.

I would be firm less often, and affirm much more.

I'd build self–esteem first, and the house later.

I'd teach less about the love of power,
and more about the power of love.

It matters not whether my child is big or small.

From this day forth, I'll cherish it all.

Diane Loomans

Contents

Heading Out

May the Lord cause you to flourish,
both you and your children.

Psalm 115:14 (NIV)

It was during our training college years that my wife, Stacie, and I announced to our friends and family that we were going to be parents. There were plenty of pats on the back, lots of *woo–hoo*'s, and multiple choruses of "Way to go! Congratulations!" At that time of joyous excitement, we had no way of knowing about the pitfalls, minefields, loss of sleep, heartaches, headaches, worries, and hurts we would experience alongside the tremendous joys, overwhelming pride, and life fulfillment we would be blessed with. To set the record straight: through all of it, I have loved, and love, being a father.

Taking on the responsibility of being a parent is like

heading out to sea. The unrelenting emotional waves toss us up and down, up and down, up and down … you get it. Children have this wonderful ability to make a parent feel simultaneously like a proud ship's captain and an abused deckhand. Every mother and father in the world who takes their responsibility of being a parent seriously gets to go on this same nonstop ride. However, as Salvation Army officers serving in a ministry that is subject to relatively frequent moves, we have the added challenge of helping our children successfully navigate the deep waters, narrow channels, and occasional storms that result from such a lifestyle.

There are three reasons why writing this book became important for me, and for my daughter, Brittany, as well. First, the process of putting the book together has been personally helpful to us in reviewing the past 22 years of life in our ministry family. I grew up in an officer family, just as my daughter has, and neither one of us responded particularly well to moving, or to the multiple life changes inherent in this type of transition. I was a high school student, an extreme introvert, when my officer parents gave me a double shock: we were moving, not to another town within our territory in the U.S, but to Africa. (Let me just say, that was quite a first day of school.) Given my own struggles with moving as an adolescent, I felt a deep, pervasive sense of guilt seeing my own child experience the same pain and loss when she was forced to move.

The second motivation for writing this book stems from a survey I conducted among all active officers in the Southern Territory. The survey was designed to discover common threads associated with officer attrition rates. The results demonstrated that a significant number of officer parents struggle with helping their children deal with moves. Of the 423 officers who responded, 211 listed children and itinerancy as their number one personal "felt need." Comments from officers who responded to the survey appear throughout this book.

In the division where my wife and I currently serve, there are many young officers. They find themselves in a season of their lives when their families are growing. It's likely that the children born to these officers will be moved multiple times along with their families. So the third motivation for writing this book is to help prepare these families for that reality. Our desire is to offer them the benefits of our seafaring experience and provide them with navigational instruments to assist them in guiding their children through the waters ahead.

Of course, not every child struggles with moving from appointment to appointment. Some flourish and even excel. Still other children adjust extremely well at one stage of life and struggle at another. There is no magic formula for knowing how our children will react to moving at each stage of life, though the experience does seem to become more emotionally taxing as children grow older. Factors that contribute to how a child will react and the time it takes to recover from a move include: the child's innate personality, age at the time of transition, siblings' reaction to the move, peer social support network, family dynamics, school experience, corps fellowship, and so on.

The Salvation Army is not unique in moving families from community to community. A 2015 report describing the U.S. population stated: "For the past several years, the mover rate has remained between 11.5 and 12.5 percent, according to new 2014 statistics released today from the U.S. Census Bureau. The mover rate between 2013 and 2014 was 11.5 percent or 35.7 million people age 1 year and over." Suffice it to say, we are a population on the move.

The difference between a ministry organization like the Army and other entities that require their personnel to make frequent moves is that we are pastors. We understand better than most the value of spiritual support and guidance through difficult life experiences. This ability and desire to pastor those who are struggling should extend to our own children first and foremost.

No one knows your child like you do. The best person to understand how well your child is coping and what is needed to help is you.

The fundamental purpose of this book is simply to bring intentional focus to our most precious earthly treasure and our first pastorate, our family. The book offers helpful ideas and a general template on which to build a specific personal plan that can best support your child. And remember, you don't have to struggle alone. Please, if you or your child needs professionally skilled help at the time of a move, immediately contact the administration. Don't let another day go by without tapping into this resource. The services the Army provides in the area of mental health and well–being are outstanding. My own family has taken advantage of this gift, to our great benefit.

Finally, I have to acknowledge a practical, but sad reality: We can be brilliant in fulfilling our parental responsibilities and upholding our children and still lose them to the world. Sometimes children can receive the very best of everything, including ourselves as parents, and still falter as adults. At the end of the day, all we can do is our very best, and then, when our children become adults, transition into loving, sometimes anxious, onlookers. Most important of all, we must pray as never before.

1

Well-Intentioned Failure

Children are a gift from the Lord.

Psalm 127:3 (CEB)

While attending college in the 1980s, my wife and I developed a terrible, shameful addiction; we became hopelessly hooked on the daytime soap opera, "Days of Our Lives." The opening musical theme along with the narrator dramatically declaring, "Like sands through the hourglass, so are the days of our lives," would start our pulses racing with eager anticipation. Each day would find us sitting on the edge of our couch ready to learn about what tragedy would next befall poor Bo and Hope, who always seemed to be the focus of some evil plot to destroy their love. What a much younger us didn't fully grasp during those carefree days was just how fleeting time truly is. No matter how much we may wish it to not be so, our children grow up as we grow old. It's an unrelenting truth that can feel as if sand is literally flowing without letup through an hourglass.

Our current season of life finds us watching our daughter build her own life independent of us. As we watch her grow into her own fully realized adult, we feel somewhat torn. On the one hand, we long to experience again our little girl who needed her daddy to help her with an elementary school project the morning it was due or wanted her mommy to make a boo–boo go away. On the other, we're glorifying God that she is successfully building her own life. Stacie and I spend a lot of time reflecting on cherished memories of Brittany during various stages of her growth, remembering the good days that the Lord provided to our family as our daughter grew and developed, as well as the challenging ones that seem to come as part of the parenting package.

Fortunately, aging has a wonderful way of helping us see the past as a stroll through a beautiful rose garden. The fact is, though, that in among the roses there have been some very painful thorns that even now can cause moments of sadness. One of these dates back to the time when our daughter was 12 years old. She was thoroughly enjoying our appointment as DYS's. (It's nice to be camp queen!) The non–Army side of life was also good. She had established some great friendships and was excelling in school. And if that wasn't enough good stuff, our appointment happened to be in our family's home town. So for the first time in our officership, Brittany found herself surrounded by her extended family. Life for her was coming up roses. Then came

The Phone Call

The news was that we were being moved from our home in the heart of the Southern Bible Belt to Southeast Florida, where real Southerners are a rare breed. I re-

> *I think that there needs to be more intentionality about officers' children. They get lost in the cracks.*
>
> *—an officer*

member with unwanted clarity the moment when I told my daughter that we were moving. As I recount it now, it still brings tears to my eyes. I knew that the announcement was going to be difficult for her, so I came to the conversation fully prepared to convince her just how wonderful this news actually was. I brought with me a quiver of "good reason for moving" arrows, including white sand beaches, Disney World, and no winter. After all, this was her fourth move as an officer's kid, and arrows like these had worked well the first three times. So why shouldn't they score another victory now?

At first, as I was breaking the news to her, Brittany didn't say a word. Then, as if in slow motion, her eyes began to fill with tears. She wasn't making a sound, but her increasing emotional pain was obvious. I immediately went on the offensive and began shooting my arrows at her again and again. But each shot seemed to only bring more hurt and bigger tears. As my arrows bounced off, I found myself at a loss. It was as if, within just a few minutes, I had utterly betrayed her. After my arrow barrage failed so miserably, I didn't know what to do or say to make her feel better. Frankly, at that moment I probably did more damage than ever with my fumbling words.

At that point in my parenting life, I didn't understand that what my daughter needed was time and space to fully grasp the news, and then time and opportunity to mourn. I also didn't realize that what I should

A parent can hurt a child by not providing the correct amount of emotional connection at the appropriate moment.

—Cloud and Townsend
Boundaries

have been concentrating on was helping her to mentally process this transition and pastoring her through her grief. I genuinely believed, quite wrongly, that my parental responsibility was to somehow eliminate the pain from my baby girl's consciousness. Given that that was clearly impossible, I was bound to fail. Looking back now, I realize that in a sense my parenting had just begun.

The most important takeaway from any moment of total failure is the simple resolve to never make the same mistake again. I vowed that I would never again come to a move conversation with my daughter equipped with only Sesame Street–inspired happy, happy, joy, joy words. In addition to researching all the cool things that a new appointment had to offer, I would approach such a conversation prepared to help her mourn the loss of her current "normal."

So how should we approach our children when they are experiencing a deep sense of hurt and loss? If a soldier came to you or me as their corps officer and shared that they were struggling because of some traumatic transition in their life, what would we do? Would we tell them that everything was going to be fine because it's God's will, and send them home? Would we tell them to just get over it? Would we diminish their sense of loss and bewilderment by telling them they shouldn't feel that way? Would we describe to them how much better off they're going to be because of what has happened? Would we question their faith level and spiritual walk because they're hurting?

I certainly hope not! We would begin the pastoring process by being fully present in the moment, listening intently as they pour out their hearts, and

Children are not a distraction from more important work. They are the most important work.

—anonymous

then loving on them. After an appropriate length of time of listening and crying with them, we'd walk slowly and tenderly beside them as they worked through the mourning process along the road to recovery. We'd likely meet and talk with them a number of times to monitor their progress and to find out if we could help them in some specific, tangible way.

If this is the right way to help someone outside our family cope with a significant loss, how much more important it is for us to apply this same recovery model to our own children for whom we have full and ultimate responsibility. If our children aren't lovingly nurtured as they should be—spiritually, emotionally, and physically—we've failed to fulfill the Pauline directive to Timothy: among the qualifications for Christian leadership is proper care for our children. Our children matter, and they are looking to us for help and hope. Let's not let them down. As they struggle to navigate the troubled waters of a stormy time in their lives, let's not let them drown.

2

Children: Our First Pastorate

Come, children, listen to me.
Let me teach you how to honor the Lord.

Psalm 34:11 (CEB)

The mission of The Salvation Army is "to preach the gospel of Jesus Christ and to meet human needs in His name without discrimination." It's natural for us as officers, ministers within the Army ranks, to identify with Kingdom work that involves helping the helpless and giving hope to the hopeless. And there are many days when it can seem much easier to reach out to the destitute and spiritually bankrupt than to pastor and lead our own families. Let's face it, raising a family is a messy business, with days full of surprises, shifting emotions, and unforeseen difficulties. Ministering to the whosoever is much more straightforward and doesn't carry with it the same emotional baggage.

Furthermore, shepherding our families doesn't garner for us the same esteem, sometimes even awe, that we tend to receive from

> *Kids are more important than reputations.*
>
> *—London and Wiseman*
> *Pastors at Greater Risk*

the community at large. In most towns and cities, our uniforms win us open access, with a high level of respect, to the rich and powerful. In contrast, our families see us as ordinary people with all our faults and foibles. This can create a temptation for us to want to live in a world of being called Captain rather than being the object of our children's rolling eyes and fits of emotion. This difference in the way we are perceived becomes particularly obvious when problems and crises flare up at home. During difficult days of familial strife, our occupation can become a safe haven for us.

Our work as officers will often provide us the perfect opportunity to justify abdication of parental time and responsibility as we devote ourselves to what God has called us to be: ministers of the Gospel. After all, Abraham was accounted a great man of faith because he was willing to place his son Isaac on the altar of sacrifice.

But unless God explicitly tells us to sacrifice our children on the altar of service to Him, the primary focus of our calling must be to care for them and pastor them.

In his first letter to Timothy, Paul sets forth in straightforward terms God's expectations of us as parents, making it clear that if our own households aren't properly taken care of and in good order, we don't qualify to be Salvation Army officers. Paul writes, *"Church officials must be in control of their own families, and they must see that their children are obedient and always respectful. If they don't know how to control their own families, how can they look after God's people?"* 1 Timothy 3:4–5 (CEV)

The Greek word that is translated *control* here can also be interpreted as *manage, put before, set over,* even *rule.* We are responsible for effectively leading and overseeing our children's conduct and well–being before we can be

> *It is the responsibility of parents to nurture and guide the spiritual life of their children.*
>
> *—Orders and Regulations for Officers*

considered worthy of overseeing and leading a church. If our families are, to use a popular phrase, a "hot mess," we must attend to fixing our family issues before we can look toward helping others address their issues.

A key Old Testament text—the central text of the Torah and of all Jewish religious life—provides an essential foundation for effective godly parenting. It begins with the "Shema," which is the first word of the passage, meaning, "hear" or "listen." Even in our time, observant Jews reverently quote the "Shema" passage at least once a day.

> *'Hear, O Israel: The Lord our God, the Lord is one! You shall love the Lord your God with all your heart and with all your soul and with all your might.'* Deuteronomy 6:4–5 (ESV)

The text goes on to say: *"And these words that I command you today shall be on your heart. You shall teach them diligently to your children, and shall talk of them when you sit in your house, and when you walk by the way, and when you lie down and when you rise."* Deuteronomy 6:6–7 (ESV) This passage is fundamental not only for Jewish life, but also for Christian life. God charges believing parents to teach their children to love God above all else and to walk in His way. That teaching is not to be an occasional thing, but is to be done consistently, on a daily basis.

Jesus made a remarkable statement about children.

> *The disciples came to Jesus and asked, 'Who is the greatest in the kingdom of heaven?'*

Then he called a little child over to sit among the disciples, and said, 'I assure you that if you don't turn your lives around and become like this little child, you will definitely not enter the kingdom of heaven. Those who humble themselves like this little child will be the greatest in the kingdom of heaven. Whoever welcomes one such child in my name welcomes me. As for whoever causes these little ones who believe in me to trip and fall into sin, it would be better for them to have a huge stone hung around their necks and be drowned in the bottom of the lake.... Be careful that you don't look down on one of these little ones. I say to you that their angels in heaven are always looking into the face of my Father who is in heaven.' Matthew 18:1–6, 10 (CEB)

It's clear that children are very important to God. The angels who watch over them have priority access to Him! I believe the reason for Jesus' stern warning against causing a child to stumble spiritually is that children are so impressionable and quick to follow an adult's leading. If we don't set a godly example for our children, we are imposing an ungodly impression on them that will last a lifetime. Don't think for a moment that this means only the children in our corps. It also refers to those living within our house.

Prioritizing the care and guidance of our children might seem to be nothing more than following a straightforward, simple recipe, a

> *Children have never been very good at listening to their elders, but they have never failed to imitate them.*
>
> —James Baldwin
> *Nobody Knows My Name*

"no–brainer." However, the reality of the immense day–to–day responsibilities we carry as officers can make it extremely difficult to establish proper family priorities and then follow through on a consistent basis. It can be easy for us to become overwhelmed with helping others and meeting organizational expectations, particularly during the Christmas season—a pivotal time for the work, but also the ultimate time of excitement for children. Every Army officer is at least periodically overcome by the demands of the congregants, the community, and the organization. That means we have to be intentional and strategic in making room for our children, even between kettle runs or council meetings. We can't allow our ministry busyness to eclipse our responsibility to love God first and to minister as we should to our in–house pastorate: our children.

If reflecting on our own parenting history makes us

realize that we've been great at the business of ministry but faltering with family relational time, feelings of guilt and discouragement are the worst possible reaction. The Lord is always waiting for us to be a Mary rather than being the best Martha in the room. Whatever parenting mistakes we've made in the past, today can be a brand–new start. Beginning with this moment, we can be what our children need us to be, no matter how old they are.

Please don't misunderstand what I'm saying. A family–first pastoring/parenting model isn't an excuse to disregard the other ministries of our officership. It's simply a call to prioritize, to put our responsibilities in proper order. Consider this truth: the healthier and better adjusted our families are, and the deeper their spiritual relationship with God is, the more time and energy we will have to minister to the least and the lost. What good are we to the least and the lost if we're experiencing spiritual

> *Officership is a very busy vocation. We are often away from our children and families for days and weeks at a time. At the same time, there is pervasive pressure to tend to the needs of the corps/command. On occasion, I need someone to tell me 'Family First' and mean it.*
>
> *—an officer*

bankruptcy and burnout at home, or the physical and mental exhaustion that results from attempting to work through the problems caused by our own failure to properly address the needs of our children?

As parents, in addition to being responsible for the training, care, and nurturing of our children, we are called to be an example of godly living. This becomes all the more important when our young ones are experiencing one of life's inevitable challenges, including the difficulties associated with being moved along with their parents from appointment to appointment. Proper care and guidance, based on tender love, will increase the likelihood that our children can be an asset to our ministries and not a detraction because of anxiety and strife. We need to be constantly aware that our particular ministry lifestyle can and does bring disruption to our children's lives. We need to always be preparing for those moments of upheaval by helping our children understand that for us, they are an uppermost priority.

In a book she titled *Tender Roses,* Lisa Wingate wrote: "Your children are the greatest gift God will give to you, and their souls the heaviest responsibility He will place in your hands. Take time with them, teach them to have faith in God. Be a person in whom they can have faith. When you are old, nothing else you've done will have mattered as much."

PRAYER OVER OUR CHILDREN

God, this world is hostile.

And sometimes violence and pain
fall on good and innocent people.

As parents we see this and the insecurity
these threats spark in us are sometimes immobilizing.

We cannot insure the safety of our own children.

Our reach is too short, and we can never even
anticipate all the risks they might face.

Often our imaginations run wild.

Our fears for our children
and for ourselves seeing our children in
danger or pain can overwhelm us.

God, when we come to the end of our ability
to control things, we turn to you.

We ask for your protection over our children,
over their choices, over the friends they make,
over the encounters they have with other adults.

God, stand guard.

Don't Let Them Drown

We do not always understand
how your protection works,
and why some who call to you are
seemingly not kept safe.

Still, we ask for your presence in the lives of our kids.

Who else can we trust, but you?
We certainly cannot secure their lives ourselves.
And you do promise to guard and protect when we ask.

'The Lord is my refuge and strength,
an ever present help in trouble.'

This is the promise we claim for our children.
Be ever present with them, and keep them
from danger and sickness and violence and
foolishness and accidents of nature.

Send angels to be beside them today.

AMEN

Mark Herringshaw

3

Pulling Up and Replanting

Jesus took the children in his arms and blessed them by placing His hands on them.

Mark 10:15–16 (CEV)

It's probably not paradigm–shifting or earth–shattering news to any officer to say that moving is difficult under the best of circumstances. We all know that moving with only six weeks' notice causes our family, adults and children both, a high level of stress. Six weeks isn't much time in which to make a successful transition, considering everything we have to do at the corps, in the office, in the community, with properties, and with our family. Very little time is left for parents to properly analyze their children's reaction to the news that a move is about to take place and then do everything possible to try and ensure a healthy emotional transition for them.

This means that we must anticipate the needs of our children and begin the process of addressing those needs long before we receive that fateful call on that special morning. It's while we're still living in the "calmer days" (I can hear you snickering about the thought of "calmer days.") that we must lay the foundation for pastoring our children through the inevitable change to come.

Let's begin with a basic understanding of the science behind how the moving process affects each one of us. This should help us as parents to understand what our children—and, in reality, we ourselves—are feeling. The difference between our children and ourselves is that our maturity and past experience make us more readily capable of dealing with these intense emotions.

The Emotional/Relational Flow Chart [on the next page] offers a general representation of what many people experience during the phases of the move cycle.

Transition: Emotional/Relational Flow Chart

Time Frame	Current Appointment	Farewell Orders	The Move	Initial Time in New Appointment	Re–Established in New Appointment
Social Posture	Committed - Involved - Belonging - Bonding - Vision	Distancing - Loosen ties - Disengage - Withdraw	Chaos - Loss of relationships - Isolation - Exaggerate problems	Superficial - Observer - Uncertain - Exaggerated behavior - Risk taking	Committed - Involved - Belonging - Bonding - Vision
Social Status	Belonging - Part of group - Position - Respect	Celebration - Attention - Recognition - Farewells - Closure	Statusless - Loss of friends - Loss of role - Loss of community	Introducing - Marginal - Who can I trust?	Belonging - Part of group - Position - Respect
Emotional Experience	Intimacy -Secure -Affirmed -Bonded	Denial - Rejection - Resentment - Sadness - Guilt	Anxiety - Grief from loss - Anger - Panic - Emotional instability	Vulnerable - Fearful - Ambivalent - Easily offended - Guarded	Intimacy - Secure - Affirmed - Bonded

The Current Appointment

At the left of the chart, in our "Current Appointment," our children have settled into a sense of normalcy that conveys feelings of stability and belonging. These comfortable feelings exist regardless of whether or not our children like every aspect of our appointment.

As our children grow and develop, one of their primary needs is for a peer group, a social support network. Ideally, even when a child falls in and out of

> *We need relationships.*
> *We need enduring,*
> *intimate bonds; we need*
> *to be able to confide;*
> *we need to feel like we*
> *belong; we need to be*
> *able to get support—and*
> *just as important for*
> *happiness, we need to be*
> *able to give support.*
>
> —Gretchen Rubin
> *Psychology Today online*

individual friendships, there is some consistency in this social sphere. Being part of a stable group of friends provides an assurance of continuity and affirmation.

A second primary need our children have is for security. Security means, first and foremost, physical safety. But it also includes a stable home with a loving parent or parents and familiarity with the physical environment. Mundane things are important to children in knowing that their world is controlled and protected: the color of their room, the feeling of the bed they sleep in, the location of the bathroom in relation to their bedroom, how big the yard is, the route to school, where their classroom is located within the school, where the nearest pizza place is, what the corps looks like, and so on and on.

Farewell Orders

Suddenly, everything that's "normal" gets put on a timetable for destruction. For the next six weeks, as plans are made, boxes appear, items disappear, and briefs are written, we have to be on guard

As a mother, I find myself missing out on the needs of our children. They are often home alone because of school activities vs corps duties.

—an officer

against the possibility that our children become nothing more than a sideline we deal with on a "needs–only" basis, focused on *our* needs. In other words: *I* need you to pack, *I* need you to take this note to school, *I* need you to be ready for this corps farewell meeting. If our children are our first pastorate, it's vital that we are intentional about carefully and thoughtfully addressing their emotional needs, even if the doughnuts are late for the morning staff farewell.

Let's look at the second column in the chart, titled "Farewell Orders." During those six weeks, there is a symphony of emotional upheaval. On the one hand, our children get to be the center of attention. In addition to the public farewells, their friends express their feelings about the one who is leaving them, going out into the great beyond. On the other hand, as each day goes by, an increasing realization grows within them that every-thing they see and experience as their "normal" is com-ing to an end. The known becomes the unknown, and our children find themselves trying to figure out how to deal with separating from their friends and their familiar environment. From their perspective, they're powerless in the face of this building wave that is sweeping them along, waiting to crash over them.

In addition to their own emotional upheaval, our children now find themselves in the position of being the cause of their friends' feelings of loss. How does our middle–school child say to a best friend, "I'm leaving you and I won't be coming back?" This is especially dif-ficult if our children's friends have never moved them-selves. Or what if our children's friends start to shut them out as a defense mechanism against being hurt? And batten down the hatches and put on the life jackets if your child is "in love"! This kind of loss can seem to a child like the literal end of the world. If a love interest is involved, the need for care and sensitivity toward your child increases exponentially.

A study published in the *Journal of Social and Per-sonality Psychology* found:

> Frequent moves are tough on kids and disrupt
> important friendships. These effects are most

problematic for kids who are introverted and those whose personalities tend toward anxiety and inflexibility.... Adults who moved frequently as kids have fewer high quality relationships and tend to score lower on well–being and life satisfaction.

Therefore, our actions today are important not only for the moment, but also for the lifelong emotional health and happiness of our children. An online publication of the American Academy of Child and Adolescent Psychiatry states,

> Moving to a new community may be one of the most stress–producing experiences a family faces. Frequent moves or even a single move can be especially hard on children and adolescents. Studies show children who move frequently are more likely to have problems at school. Moves are even more difficult if accompanied by other significant changes in the child's life, such as a death, divorce, loss of family income, or a need to change schools.

*Teenagers have a rough
time with moves and
all that goes on
with officer life.*

—*an officer*

This last point relates to the question of the age at which the move experience is hardest on a child. The study in the *Journal of Social and Personality Psychology* mentioned above also indicated that "Moves are hardest on kids in the midst of other transitions, like puberty and school changes. Middle school seems to be the toughest time to make a transition." But the emotional impact a move has on a specific child is as individualized as our children are. In my family, for example, our daughter is currently in her 20s and attends college 12 states away, yet our moves still affect her sense of security.

The Move

When we slide one step to the right in the flow chart, under the heading, "The Move," we see that the breaking of our children's normal life creates an elevated level of anxiety that can involve loss, isolation, and grief. In many cases, children will try, with good intentions, to hold onto their past friendships through online and phone connections. At first this may seem to be somewhat successful, but with school–age children the old adage "out of sight, out of mind" proves true. As past friends share new experiences with their peers in the previous appointment, they will slowly but surely disengage from their ties with our child. This distancing is especially painful for our children if they haven't begun the process of establishing a peer social support network of their own in the new appointment.

My daughter experienced this firsthand. Soon after our move to the Sunshine State, her previous best friend from school participated in a field trip to Disney's MGM Studios in Orlando. As Brittany had not yet established a firm footing with a peer group in our new appointment, this opportunity seemed ready-made for a respite from her loneliness. So off to MGM we went. The day with Movie Mickey was far from helpful. Brittany's best friend was working hard to establish a new relationship with another girl, which left our daughter out in the cold. The experience actually increased Brittany's feelings of loneliness and deepened her resentment about moving. I watched this tragedy unfold in slow motion and felt as completely helpless as I'd ever felt in our daddy–daughter relationship. I was at a complete loss as to what I could do to help heal her emotional wounds, which

> *I need tools for my daughter in handling a move.*
>
> *—an officer*

were being watered with tears that none of us could have predicted would dominate that fateful day.

My intention in sharing all this information is not to present a picture of inevitable doom. What I hope for instead is that we as officer parents will take seriously our responsibility to pastor our children effectively for their lifelong mental health and well–being. That pastoring process begins as we take time to let our children know that they're valued and as we establish a mentally and behaviorally balanced and healthy household environment for them.

In the New Appointment

The next phase in the flow chart is where I believe we can have the greatest parental impact. Of course, the level of influence we have during this period depends on how well we've prepared for it and the quality time we've already invested in emotional support for our children. During these initial days and weeks, our children are experiencing a combination of low peer interaction, marginalization, and loneliness. The parent can step in to fill this gap to some degree but also can work to create opportunities for peer social interactions. It's critical that we be in the moment and emotionally available with our time and support during this critical phase of our children's lives.

WARNING: Drugs and alcohol

When our children are adolescents, we should be vigilant in watching for signs of experimentation with drugs or alcohol. As our children enter a brand–new school environment, we have no control over who will be the first people to befriend them. This fact, combined with our children's need for peer bonding, should make us extra cautious. If the first peers our children start to bond with are experimenting with mood–altering substances, our children's need to fit in or establish a new social support group may override their established convictions. Experimentation with illicit substances is likely to result in our children withdrawing even further from us because of their sense of guilt. Stay involved and, without being excessively intrusive, know who your child is bonding with.

Re-established

"I've found a new friend." When we finally hear these longed–for words, we know our child has started to enter the final column of the chart: being emotionally re–established in the new appointment. That first peer connection can be the launching point from which our children can blossom and rebuild their very important social support network. Over time, hopefully, they will find themselves fully bonded with new friends, once again experiencing that sense of belonging and being comfortable in their new environment. The time it takes for this re–establishment varies greatly, but for every-one's sake you hope it happens sooner than later.

Our ultimate goal as parents is to help our children find their way into the emotional state of normalcy at the far right of the chart. We can't force a sense of comfort and security, but we can provide every opportunity pos-sible to facilitate it. I imagine there are some children who never fully find their way back to complete emo-tional and social re–establishment. For these children, prolonged isolation and loneliness can leave deep and long–lasting emotional scars. If you have a child who is finding it particularly difficult to make the leap, or one who can't seem to make a successful transition even after a significant period of time has passed, please seek out professionally skilled help. At the very least, a single professional assessment

> *I need pastoral care in helping my child adjust to the Army lifestyle.*
>
> —an officer

can make a world of difference in providing tools for their adjustment.

Once a normal state has been re–established, guess what? It's likely to be just a matter of time before the phone rings again, even if we're hoping that that time is as far off as possible. So we need to be prepared for the next storm over the horizon. Once we're fully established, our new appointment becomes the new left–hand column of the transition flow chart. We can best prepare for this expected upheaval by creating an atmosphere in our household that maximizes our children's feelings of stability and sets a firm foundation on which to stand when the emotional maelstrom threatens once more to engulf us.

MEMO FROM A CHILD

Don't spoil me. I know quite well
that I ought not to have all I ask for.

Don't be afraid to be firm with me.
I prefer it, it makes me feel secure.

Don't let me form bad habits.
I have to rely on you
to detect them in the early stages.

Don't make me feel smaller than I am. It only
makes me behave stupidly "big."

Don't correct me in front of people
if you can help it. I will take
much more notice if you talk
quietly to me in private.

Don't make me feel that my mistakes are sins.
It upsets my sense of values.

Don't protect me from consequences.
I need to learn the painful way sometimes.

Don't be upset when I say, "I hate you." It isn't you
I hate but your power to thwart me.

Don't take too much notice of my small ailments.
Sometimes they get me the attention I need.

Don't nag. If you do, I shall have to
protect myself by appearing deaf.

Don't forget that I cannot explain myself
as well as I should like. That is why
I am not always accurate.

Don't put me off when I ask questions.
If you do you will find that I'll stop asking
and I'll seek my information elsewhere.

Don't be inconsistent. That completely
confuses me and makes me lose faith in you.

Pulling Up and Replanting

Don't tell me my fears are silly.
They are terribly real and you can
do much to reassure me if you try to understand.

Don't ever suggest that you are perfect or
infallible. It gives me too great a shock when
I discover that you are neither.

Don't ever think that it is beneath your dignity to
apologize to me. An honest apology makes me
surprisingly warm towards you.

Don't forget how quickly I am growing up.
It must be very difficult for you to keep pace
with me but please do try.

Don't forget that I don't thrive without
lots of love and understanding,
but I don't need to tell you, do I?

anonymous

4

How Much Is
Too Much?

Parents, don't provoke your children
in a way that ends up discouraging them.

Colossians 3:21 (CEB)

B eing a parent is an exciting adventure. Few experiences in life can be compared to the personal joy
and swelling pride we feel when our children receive
recognition for significant achievements. When my
daughter was in elementary school, she decided she
wanted to play soccer. She insisted that I join her so that
we could share in the experience, and I was very glad
to do that. Being a dutiful father, I went to the soccer
sign–ups and volunteered to help as a secondary coach.
What I didn't know was that they were running short of

coaches, so—congratulations!—I was presented with a team of my very own.

Well, my daughter was a terrible player and I was an even worse coach. That's not to say that we didn't have a great time. We actually had a blast. But my team wasn't one to be feared. My clearest memory of that entire season was the one goal my daughter somehow scored. For that one glorious moment, I was the greatest coach and dad of the most spectacularly athletic daughter ever to enter the world of AYSO soccer. I don't even remember whether we won or lost the match. All that mattered to me was that my child had been successful for that one moment.

Unfortunately, there is a dark underside to child rearing that confronts us when our children struggle or fail in some way. When these hurtful moments arise, we as parents share the pain, sometimes feeling it even more acutely than our children. It's especially tough when our children experience hurts that we feel helpless to address. During these difficult days, the best gift we can offer is emotional support, being available and always ready with a loving and comforting hug.

In addition to the natural parental cycle of emotional ebbs and flows, we as officers also experience years of accentuated undulating emotions emanating from appointment transfers. I recall clearly the feeling of relief that washed over my wife, Stacie, and me when our daughter graduated from high school. For the first time in 18 years we didn't have to worry about the impact our moving was going to have on her. What a relief! Until that milestone is reached, however, officer parents need to pay close attention to their children's behaviors, emotional states, and general attitudes. This is especially true during the time period between the farewell orders phone call and their re–connection with a new peer social support group in the new appointment. Vigilant monitoring, discernment, and wisdom gained from experience are the best tools we have for being able to know how to help our children and deciding whether professional intervention might be warranted.

As I was growing up, my father was a stern man; he had lived life on the hard road. One result was that whenever someone around him experienced physical or mental pain, his response was, "Get up! You aren't hurt." I'll never forget the day as a kid when I was throwing a baseball with him in the yard and one of his throws pegged me directly in the eye. I cried, my eye turned black, my brother laughed, my mother freaked out, and my dad said, "That'll teach you to keep your glove up." In his world, admitting to any personal need was seen as weakness, which men just didn't show. I don't blame him for his parental approach. That was how he'd been raised and all he knew. But it's incumbent upon us as officer parents to be sensitive to our children's needs and to address them with wisdom and discernment in a loving manner.

Most children suffer some degree of emotional distress during a move and will exhibit out–of–character behavior. They typically display their feelings in ways that are fairly obvious: withdrawal, anger, aggressiveness, sadness, and so on. With many children, these reactions can be addressed by creating a personal plan designed for just that purpose and following that plan when the need arises.

> My oldest child has learning difficulties, which affect other areas as well. I would like some help with that as well as general parenting issues.
>
> —an officer

(A personal plan template is provided and discussed in a later chapter). In other words, we shouldn't pick up on an indicator of distress, especially during the first couple of days after a move, and launch ourselves into panic mode. It takes us as adults some time to process the transition from one appointment to another. So let's give our children the courtesy of patiently watching, listening, and then helping them through their own transition process.

Superhero Parents

When I was a child, I collected comic books. My personal favorites were Dr. Strange and Thor. I would spend hours daydreaming about what it would be like to have a superpower, a special ability that far exceeds that of any ordinary person. The superhero uses that special ability to come to people's rescue when they are facing an insurmountable problem.

As the adult in our family group, we're in possession of the superpowers of elevated levels of maturity, experience, and knowledge. We can embrace a superhero role in our children's lives and use these advantages in creating and applying ideas for alleviating their distress. We should never sink to our child's level of negative outbursts and emotional fits while we're trying to help them successfully navigate through their problems. We can help our children best when we display maturity—disregarding our pride and insecurities and staying focused on addressing their needs.

Here's an example. After moving to a new appointment, a child withdraws into his room and refuses to go to Wednesday night

> *My children are growing frustrated with the demands on our family.*
>
> *—an officer*

Bible study. Our blood pressure rises and our anger starts to swell in response to the obstinate attitude. How do we react? Do we become aggressive and shout out threats about the punishments we're going to visit on him? Do we meekly slink away and avoid the situation because we want our child to like us? Neither of these approaches is very helpful. Our children act and react based on what they perceive as solid reasoning. The key for us as superhero parents is to use our special abilities to create a safe, comfortable environment. First, we consider the child's reasons for not wanting to go. Then we use that information to negotiate an agreeable resolution for everyone involved. It probably won't happen that very evening, but we're not looking for short–term victories; we're looking for lifetime balance.

You may be thinking: *How in the world can I keep myself in check when my child is throwing a royal temper tantrum and accusing me of being a horrible parent?* There are some great books available on conflict resolution. A couple I've enjoyed reading are *The Eight Essential Steps to Conflict Resolution* by Dudley Weeks and *Fierce Conversations* by Susan Scott.

In her book, Dr. Scott presents a simple structure for a parent/child conversation in a difficult situation:

- Name the issue.
- Select a specific example that illustrates the be-havior you want to have changed.
- Describe your emotions about this issue.
- Clarify what is at stake.
- Identify openly what your contribution to this problem has been.
- Indicate your wish to resolve the issue.
- Invite your child to respond.

I've added one more item:

- Listen to what your child is saying and take it seriously.

Don't be afraid to suspend the conversation if you need some time to cool off. Your children will push you as far as they can, and it's up to us as parents to use our superpowers of maturity, experience, and knowledge to control our own anger, which helps to set the boundaries of the conflict.

Stress Indicators

For some children, a move will be accompanied by an extreme level of stress. This can generally be identified in one of two different ways: (1) The child exhibits argumentative or aggressive behaviors toward others or even toward themselves. (Note: If your child is causing or threatening to cause harm to themselves or others, this is a clear indicator that professional help is needed immediately.) (2) The child withdraws from social interaction or demonstrates depression or sadness. Introverts will typically tend to turn inward, whereas extroverts will tend to lash outward.

Allow children to express grief, loss, or sadness without trying to cheer them up and talk them out of their feelings.

—Cloud and Townsend Boundaries

The word "extreme" is important here. Many children will exhibit these behaviors; it's a matter of degree. If you're looking for a mathematical equation, begin with a baseline of what you would consider normal behavior for your child. Add to that an elevated factor for the emotional distress that a move creates. The result should be a range of expected behavior. You can then discern whether or not your child's behavior fits within this expected range. Over time, any heightened negative behaviors should slowly return to their expected normal. If they don't, professional intervention may be warranted.

Scholastic *Parents* offers eight indicators for determining whether or not a school age child is under too much stress:

1. Nightmares

2. Trouble concentrating and completing schoolwork

3. Increased aggression

4. Bedwetting

5. Hyperactive behavior

6. Withdrawing from family and friends

7. Eating or sleeping disorders

8. Overreactions to minor problems

I've added two more indicators to the list:

9. Loss of passion for key interests

10. Throughout the lives of our children, their interests may change. At one stage of their lives, they might be pursuing music; at another, some type of sport. However, if a child's enthusiasm for such a pursuit suddenly comes to a screeching halt, we need to be on the alert and look for other related signs of anxiety and stress.

11. Depression

 If a child seems listless or overly emotional or displays feelings of hopelessness, we need to pay attention and consider whether professional intervention may be warranted.

Professional Help

When a move from appointment to appointment causes the normal emotional ups and downs of our child's everyday life to be exacerbated or highly exaggerated, the worst thing we as parents can do is overreact. Accentuated negative behaviors and emotional outbursts created by the stress of a move will normally tend to lessen in severity over time toward a new normal.

In extreme cases, however, when a child's behavior seems to be far outside the norm, the question may arise: *Do we need to seek professional help?* This question is difficult to deal with, particularly if two parents have different perceptions of the emotional state of the child. For example, one parent may see frequent temper tantrums as a serious problem, while the other sees this behavior as a manifestation of independence. The ideal situation, of course, is when two parents—both carefully monitoring their child—are on the same page regarding what is acceptable behavior under the circumstances.

Unless we as parents have advanced knowledge of psychology, it can be very hard to know when to bring in professional help. What is the proper time? Sharon Brehm offered three indicators that can aid in deciding whether a child's behavior is a sign that professional help is called for:

- The duration of a troublesome behavior

  Virtually every child experiencing a move will exhibit some heightened level of abnormal emotional stress. Once the initial shock has passed, the parent should closely monitor any negative behaviors. If they don't subside over time, professional intervention may be needed. For example, if a child locks herself in her room and refuses to go to school after a few weeks in the new appointment, this is clearly detrimental to the child, and something will need to be done to help her. This something may be a visit to the school counselor, having a professional assessment completed, or perhaps considering another school. What's important in this situation is that we take positive steps toward mitigating this behavior.

- ## The intensity of the behavior

  Showing signs of withdrawal and loneliness is normal when a child arrives in a new community. The question is what level of emotional disruption is normal and expected behavior. If we've moved into a new quarters and our child is physically lashing out at others or himself, professional intervention may well be appropriate.

- ## The age of the child

  A 2–year–old child is expected to act out as a "terrible two." Similar behavior is entirely unacceptable in an 8– or 16–year–old. If a child is acting out in a way that is age–inappropriate, that's certainly something that will need to be monitored and, if severe or long–lasting enough, may require professional help.

Is there a chance of allowing more flexibility for officers with young children?

—an officer

Child psychology isn't an exact science with specific formulas to follow. Some would suggest that it's more art than science. As parents, we need to give our children some time for adjustment after a move and monitor them for improvements. If you perceive that your child is not coping well within the new environment over a period of time, and you think that an assessment with a Christian counselor may be in order, listen to your intuition and reach out. It's a balancing act: You don't want to overreact to your child's response to moving, but please don't underreact either. Your child's long–term emotional stability is at stake.

Parental Pride

The minute we decide that our child needs professional help of some sort, we may experience feelings of failure. This is especially painful if we come from a family where seeking professional help is believed to be only for the weak, or for people without enough faith. After all, our God heals, so all that's really needed is more faith—right? God does heal body and soul, but sometimes He uses doctors to carry out this work. If we as parents will go to a doctor or dentist for physical repairs and treatment, how is going to a Christian counselor or psychologist any different? Except, of course, that the wounds may be unseen and not detectable by an X–ray or a CT scan. The fact that a child may need to have professional help doesn't equal personal or parental failure.

Officer parents may be hesitant to reach out for pro-fessional help due to the fear of being labeled. They may be afraid that if they or their families demonstrate any perceived weakness, they'll be seen by the organization as a failure. Responses to the officer survey referred to in Chapter 1 were littered with comments

> *I feel that if I sought pastoral help from Administration it might reflect poorly on my ability to handle pressure, thus influencing any future appointments. This fear may be unfounded, but perceived nonetheless.*
>
> *—an officer*

showing that this is a very real fear among our fellow servants. One sad statement represents many, many others: "I trust no one in The Salvation Army. When you do feel that you can trust someone, then you hear them telling tales of other people. Well, you just never know when they too may have complete influence over you, your family, and your well–being. So you just go along. Alone in your frustrations."

When the long–term mental health of our children is in the balance, how much does it matter if we were to be labeled? And what does such a label really mean—

that we are parents who discerned a need and acted on it for the betterment of our family? We should be proud to wear such a label.

The Salvation Army offers a great program to help officers and their families deal with emotional issues. This program has been a tre-

I'm extremely thankful for the professional counseling being offered to me and my family.

—an officer

mendous help to my family in maintaining good personal and familial balance. We will always feel indebted to the Arny for this help. If our children need professional intervention and we don't seek it out for them, how can we look God in the face and say that we have been faithful stewards of these precious gifts of life that He has bestowed upon us?

Cast a mold of life and love

The hopes and dreams you're thinking of

A world so big for one so small

The sky, the trees, a big red ball

Soon to crawl, and then to walk

Soon to dream, and then to talk

Don't Let Them Drown

I have a name, I know I'm me

I taste, I feel, I hear, and see

I wrote my name at school today

I'm learning games the kids all play

I rode my bike with just two wheels

I fell and know how bad it feels

The tests to pass to graduate

The job for which I could not wait

He's all grown up I hear them say

It seems like only yesterday

Anonymous

5

Introvert, Extrovert, or Just Shy

I have calmed and quieted my soul,
like a weaned child with its mother;
like a weaned child is my soul within me.

Psalm 131:2 (ESV)

N ine o'clock at night in our household used to mean that it was time for our little one to go off to bed. Bedtime included a nightly ritual of reading multiple books with an occasional game thrown into the mix. One of the games we enjoyed most revolved around Winnie–the–Pooh and his friends. The object of the game was to take one of these characters through the Hundred–Acre Wood, collecting treasures along the way. It was a fun game, but probably not the best one to play before bed, as it got very exciting, which caused little Brittany to lose any interest she might have had in sleeping. As we were both laughing loudly because I was losing—again—her mother was yelling down the hallway that it was time to go to sleep.

The characters living in the Hundred–Acre Wood, who might be thought of as Christopher Robin's kids, provide great fodder for personality study. There is clinically depressed Eeyore; the compulsively shy Piglet; the extroverted Tigger; and, of course, the introverted leader, Pooh himself. Many authors and experts have recognized this fact and have produced such books as *Pooh and the Psychologists*, *Pooh and the Philosophers*, *Positively Pooh*, and many others.

Let's look at the personality traits of three of these characters. Understanding those traits can help to illustrate possible approaches to helping each one re–establish a peer social support structure if their "dad" received farewell orders and they were moved away from the Hundred–Acre Wood.

Piglet: Compulsively Shy

'It is hard to be brave,' said Piglet, sniffing slightly,
'when you're only a Very Small Animal.'

We've all experienced a social setting at some point in our lives in which we felt completely out of place or intimidated, producing a shy reaction. Depending on personality and circumstance, people can experience moments of shyness just once in a while or on a continuing basis. If this type of social anxiety becomes debilitating, professional intervention may be called for.

In their book *Painfully Shy*, Barbara and Gregory Markway define social anxiety this way: "It's the experience of apprehension or worry from the possibility, either real or imagined, that one will be evaluated or judged in some manner by others." Social anxiety is rooted in a fear of embarrassment or of becoming the focus of unwanted attention. Even very young children can feel an overwhelming sense of social anxiety that in extreme cases may manifest as stomachache, rapid heartbeat, headache, nausea, or shortness of breath. If your child is experiencing high levels of social anxiety, forcing a great deal of exposure to social settings can result in negative behaviors such as angry outbursts or withdrawal.

Piglet is quite shy and timid. He sees himself as small and helpless and depends on others for security and comfort. In some social situations, he may suffer from "stage fright." On the other hand, he can be very brave. He showed his courage when he held on tight to his kite string as he was blown away by the wind.

So how would Piglet react to his "father" being transferred to a new appointment, away from the Hundred–Acre Wood? His shyness might have him sitting in a corner at his new school, trying not to be noticed. His anxiety would be aggravated by his tendency to stutter, which he wouldn't want to have exposed around new people. It's possible that Piglet would spend a significant period of time secretly struggling with loneliness. This would be particularly painful for him because of his longing to be part of a peer group.

One of the best things Christopher Robin could do for Piglet is create opportunities for peer interaction. This would be easier to accomplish for a younger Piglet than for an older teenage version, who might not react well to parental interference. An idea that might work well is an interactive event revolving around Piglet's chief hobby, kite flying. This would require the commitment of some resources, as Christopher might need to buy several kites as well as a variety of picnic foods. Once the necessary items have been secured, invitations to neighborhood, corps, or school peers to "Come Fly a Kite" should be prepared. The expense and effort of the event will be more than worth it if it results in friendships for shy Piglet. The goal is to break through his shyness by creating controlled opportunities for fun peer interaction.

Winnie-the-Pooh: Introvert

'Think it over, think it under.'

Pooh

Shyness is an emotional reaction to a particular environment. In contrast, introversion is the result of hardwiring of the brain. Introversion is not a singular social reaction, but a state of being. One way of thinking about it is this: What fills or drains my internal energy reserves? For an introvert, private personal time is important for filling emotional reserves, whereas a social gathering will drain it.

At this point, without apology, I must admit to a bias. I am a card–carrying member of the Introverts of the World personality club. Our club has many very famous, successful members, including Bill Gates, Michael Jordan, Laura Bush, Steve Martin, and Michele Pfeiffer. Studying introversion has helped me understand why my particular personality trait made transitioning as an officer's child more difficult. This same introverted hardwiring was passed down to my daughter, Brittany, and I watched as she also struggled with moving.

Let me show my bias colors more fully and say that although we introverts struggle with some social aspects of life, we also have some great attributes. Marti Olsen Laney writes that introverts have "the capacity for depth, self–awareness, and close relationships." On the other hand, in the area of friendships, we tend to be a mile deep and an inch wide. That is, we need only a very few close friends, but tend to build very deep relationships with them.

> *I am an introvert by nature. The soldiery has expressed that they need me to spend more time outside of the corps programs socializing with them. On most days, by the time I address pressing needs at the corps, I only want to go home and rest/ refuel at my own leisure.*
>
> *—an officer*

This results in deeper feelings of hurt and loss when relationships are broken and increases the amount of time required to establish close connections with new friends. Introverts also have trouble handling real or perceived public embarrassment. Progress made in the formation of new relationships can vanish in an instant if they feel humiliated in any way. It's kind of like what happens when you startle a turtle. It will retreat into its shell, and it takes some time for it to re–emerge.

Introverts tend to be self–reflective and self–correcting, continually analyzing their world. This creates a need for introverts to spend quality time alone in which to observe and make sense of the people around them and of the environment. After a move, introverted children must be allowed space and time to construct a mental model of their new "normal." In working with them, we don't try to "fix" them; we create strategies that allow for both self–reflection and low–stress social interactions.

Let's have a little fun and dive into some conjecture. Pooh has just moved along with his "dad" to a new appointment in a forest far away from the Hundred–Acre Wood. What can Christopher do to help him after the move? Shy Piglet needed his "father" to create controlled opportunities for interaction with new people. Being an introvert, Pooh has different requirements. Remember that he has just lost his deeply loved close friends. As a self–reflective, self-correcting bear, before anything else he needs quality reflection time to analyze his new environment. What Christopher shouldn't do is force Pooh into social situations before he's ready. That would only serve to drain his emotional energies, which have already been brought to a low state by the move itself.

After an appropriate amount of time, Christopher will

watch Pooh carefully for signs that he is ready to branch out into small, controlled peer activities. A key difference between Pooh and Piglet is that Piglet's activities can incorporate a larger number of participants and even be a bit of a surprise. Introverts react strongly to any possibility of embarrassment, so a surprise peer event at this unsettled period in Pooh's life could prove to be counterproductive. It would be better to allow him to help in the planning and implementation of any social activity.

One great way to help Pooh settle in is by taking him on exploratory walks through the new forest. This will provide him an opportunity to define his new environment and to work through some of his emotions. Once Pooh has established a new close friend, he can be encouraged to widen his scope of interactions and activities with new people—for example, by joining his school's honey lovers club.

Intro, Extro, and Ambi

When we talk about introversion and extroversion tendencies and traits, we need to understand that, in reality, virtually each one of us has a mixture of the two. We simply fall at different points along the personality scale, [shown on next page]. A person who has an equal mixture of both kinds of traits is called an ambivert.

PERSONALITY SCALE

Introvert	Ambivert	Extrovert

When we call some-one an introvert or an extrovert, we're talking in terms of where that person fits most com-fortably on the person-ality scale according

> *There is no such thing as a pure introvert or extrovert. Such a person would be in the lunatic asylum.*
>
> *—Carl Jung*

to their innate disposition. One way of looking at the question is to think of introverts as facing inward, con-tinually analyzing themselves, their environment, and others; and extroverts as facing outward, more readily accepting other people and situations. More detailed descriptions appear in the Introvert/Extrovert Compari-son Chart [on the next page].

Introvert/Extrovert Comparison Chart

	Introverts	Extroverts
Communication Skills	Introspective and reserved. Prefers to listen.	Outgoing and talkative. Somewhat impulsive.
Emotional Walls	Easily publicly humiliated. Good at building emotional walls for protection.	Better able to cope with feelings of humiliation. Let's go of these moments more quickly.
Personal Stimulation	Seeks stimulation internally. Energized through solitude and contemplation.	Seeks stimulation externally. Energized through connections and actions.
Learning	Learns through watching and introspection.	Learns through action and experience.
Being in a Crowd	Energy–draining.	Energizing.
New Environment	Cautious	Risk taker
Change Tolerance	Craves routine and structure.	Craves external stimulation and excitement
Reaction to Intense Emotion	Draining	Energizing

Tigger: Extrovert Extraordinaire

*'Once in a while someone amazing comes along
and here I am.'*

Tigger

Tigger virtually defines the word "extrovert"—energetic, fun–loving and self–confident. Sometimes he is so overconfident that he thinks "tiggers do best" at any task, and that can get him in trouble. Tigger is not so much concerned with understanding his environment as with having a good time, so he sometimes fails to learn from his mistakes.

After all that has been said about introverts, it is easy to get the impression that extroverted children move with few or no problems. Unfortunately, this is not necessarily the case. No matter what the personality type, any child can suffer from shyness when pushed into a new environment. And every child who is moving will feel a deep sense of loss at leaving friends and familiar surroundings behind. And remember, extroverts receive much of their energy from outside themselves. With the loss of friends, an extroverted child also loses a primary source of emotional energy, outgoing as well as incoming. They may express their pent–up energy in the form of exaggerated emotional outbursts.

A distinct advantage for extroverted children when

our appointment changes can be found in the time it takes to create a new normal. They will generally re–establish a peer social support network much more quickly than an introvert will. Carefully observing our children's reaction to their new environment, regardless of personality type, is key to being able to adjust our plans in order to properly meet their needs.

Tigger has just been moved from the Hundred–Acre Wood. He's feeling a sense of hurt and loneliness because he has left behind the friends with whom he's enjoyed so many wonderful adventures. What should Christopher Robin do for him? It's important that outlets for Tigger's energy be found and opportunities for the creation of new peer friendships be provided as quickly as possible. Surprise parties and large peer gatherings can fill Tigger's needs wonderfully well. Immediate exposure to extracurricular activities could also provide a great source of emotional relief.

> *Since moving away from all my friends and family, loneliness has been at times very difficult to overcome.*
>
> —an officer

Whatever our child's innate personality may be, our primary goal after a move should be to take action in a way that best fits that child's needs. Our children are hurting, and whether they say so or not, they need us as parents to hold their hands—if not physically, certainly on an emotional level. It's vital that we help them feel a sense of stability and security in the midst of this chaotic transition. We should be thoughtfully, carefully creating whatever appropriate avenues we can for peer interaction. To leave our children sitting in their rooms alone after a move because we're not engaged is to ask for deeper and longer–lasting emotional trauma than we might imagine.

PRAYER FOR CHILDREN IN SCHOOL

Father of all mercies
we ask that you would bless
the youngest and littlest of learners,
the most helpless and powerless of persons,
with Your infinite and loving mercy.

Grant them the strength to learn,
concentrate, and act in love
towards their teachers and fellow students.

We also ask that You would watch
over them at home and at school
and give them proper direction
so that they may learn of your wonderful virtues.

AMEN

D. Bennett

6

Preparing for
the Storm

Train children in the way they should go.

Proverbs 22:6 (CEB)

The Great Galveston Hurricane of September 8, 1900, was a Category 4 storm with winds up to 145 miles per hour. The storm left some 5,000–8,000 of the city's 36,000 residents dead, making it the deadliest hurricane in U.S. history. This catastrophic loss of life was due to the extremely limited means of observation and communication available at the end of the 19th century. Ships were the only reliable means for observing hurricanes at sea, and because wireless telegraphy was in its infancy, their reports were not received until the ships put in at harbor.

On September 4, the Galveston office of the National Weather Service began receiving warnings from the bureau's central office in Washington, D.C., that a tropical storm had moved northward over Cuba. The weather bureau forecasters had no way of tracking the path of the storm; and even as they received updated information, in an effort to avoid panic, they avoided use of such terms as "hurricane" and "tornado" in their communications.

There were a couple of silver linings to this horrific storm. First, it was a significant motivator for investment by the federal government in early warning systems and preparedness. Devastating hurricanes are now an increasing reality, but warning systems and disaster planning have prevented the loss of human life on the scale that resulted from the Galveston storm. In addition, the hurricane was the catalyst for the inception of The Salvation Army's disaster response and recovery work.

A Firm Foundation

Salvation Army officers with children living at home become involved in disaster and recovery of a different kind. The reality is that we can be moved at any moment and that our children will suffer some level of loss because of these transitions. However, being prepared before the storm hits can go a long way in helping to mitigate the level of damage inflicted by the move and hasten rebuilding and recovery in our children's lives.

A determining factor in whether a building survives a major storm is the firmness of its foundation. Jesus used this as an example in His teaching:

> *'Everybody who hears these words of mine and puts them into practice is like a wise builder who built a house on bedrock. The rain fell, the floods came, and the wind blew and beat against that house. It didn't fall because it was firmly set on bedrock.'* Matthew 7:24–25 (CEB)

In preparation for the inevitable emotional storm caused by moving, we need to be working to construct a solid familial and spiritual foundation for our children while they are in a place of belonging and safety.

Because of the volume and variety of responsibilities we carry as officers, we may feel that we don't have enough time in the day for foundation building. However, for our children's sake, we have to make the time. Our children are a God–given treasure, our primary responsibility. Thomas Curtis, in his book, *Practical Wisdom for Pastors* says, "Not a congregation, not a good sermon, not a well–oiled church mechanism, but the spiritual welfare of our family must come first. Then at the end of our lives there will be no regrets!"

Unfortunately, there is no single recipe for the cement that goes into the ideal foundation. There's a lot of art mixed in with the science. Each child and every family enjoys a different dynamic, so the practical steps suggested here are necessarily general in nature. What's most important is that we understand that our children need us for more than just putting Band–Aids on boo–boos. They need our genuine and ongoing help and support in working through their emotional pain and periods of loss.

Holy Consistency

Of all the components that go into building a firm foundation for our children, none is more important—more basic—than a thoroughly Christian home. This means much more than praying before meals, watching the right kinds of videos and TV shows, and listening to Christian music. Our ultimate desire for our children, of course, is that they grow to love and serve the Lord. The best contribution we can make toward that end is not in what we say, but in what we do.

If we as parents abdicate our spiritual responsibility toward our children, we can be sure that the world is ready to fill that empty space with all manner of darkness. In the children's story "Pinocchio," a wooden boy is sent out into the world before he's been properly trained. When he encounters a fox, Pinocchio is easily manipulated and nearly destroyed. To leave a spiritual void in our children's lives is to expose them to dangerous attacks with eternal outcomes.

> *One of the most important things we as adults can do for young children is to model the kind of person we would like them to be.*
>
> —*Carol Hillman*

The most effective training tool we have is our life example. If we want our children to be godly, we have to be truly holy. Proverbs 20:7 says, *"The righteous live with integrity; happy are their children who come after them."* (CEB) The word *integrity* means more than honesty, more even than goodness; it also means consistency. Children are very good at spotting a phony, especially one who's living in the same house with them. Practical evangelism—winning our own children—requires that we live the same holy life at home that we are exhorting others to live in our Sunday sermons.

If our children perceive a spiritual disconnect between what we say and how we act, it can drive them away from true faith. I for one would never want to stand before God and explain how such a thing came to pass. I am ever mindful of these words of Jesus: *"As for whoever causes these little ones who believe in me to trip and fall into sin, it would be better for them to have a huge stone hung around their necks and be drowned in the bottom of the lake."* Matthew 18:6 (CEB)

Consider the only one of the Ten Commandments given by God in which He emphasizes unavoidable punishment: *"You shall not take the name of the Lord your God in vain, for the Lord will not leave him unpunished who takes His name in vain."* Exodus 20:7 (NASB) Two Hebrew words are key to the thrust of this commandment. The first is *nâsâ*, which has a semantic range, including "bear, carry, take." The second is *shâv*, which has a semantic range that includes "deceptive, empty, false, vain." Thus the fundamental meaning of the commandment, issued by God with a dire warning, is this: "You shall not bear the name of the Lord your God deceitfully [or falsely]." Anyone who claims to be a child of God but does not live a righteous life will not escape punishment. For your own sake and that of your children, if you're not fully saved, if you're not living a holy life, repent. Otherwise, get out of the ministry.

Taking Time to Give Time

Well, my son turned ten just the other day.
He said, 'Thanks for the ball, Dad. Come on, let's play.
Could you teach me to throw?' I said, 'Not today.
I got a lot to do.' He said, 'That's okay.'

And he walked away and he smiled and he said,
'You know, I'm gonna be like him, yeah.
You know I'm gonna be like him.'

Harry Chapin,
Cat's in the Cradle

There's an old metaphor that conceives of personal relationships as involving individual bank accounts. We're either making a deposit in the emotional account of another by giving of ourselves to them or making emotional withdrawals from them. If we have invested in the emotional account of a child, when the time comes that we need to make an emotional or relational withdrawal, there will be something to withdraw. Conversely, if we've failed to make emotional investments, when a withdrawal is truly needed, we face an empty account. Moving our children in the name of our ministry is a significant withdrawal. If we haven't been making positive investments into their lives, what can we expect to withdraw?

One of the most significant types of deposits we can make into our children's lives is quality time. When we invest time in someone, it communicates to them that they matter. We can say over and over again that we love our children, but that holds little weight if we don't support those claims by actually sacrificing our own personal time and energy in order to invest in them.

I need family time with kids, having a lunch with them and eating dinner with them on most nights.

—an officer

The gift of quality time applies to activities and actions both inside and outside the home. Eating a meal together or playing games demonstrates to our children that we value them, which promotes a sense of social belonging. Kevin Leman, in his book, *It's a Kid Not a Gerbil*, contends, "The most important thing you can give your child is your presence.… Parents—not drugs, not movies, not peer groups—are a child's number–one influence." Please take note: Spending quality time together doesn't mean sitting in the same room with a different electronic device in each person's hand. Facebooking each other across the room doesn't represent a high level of time investment in our children.

Imagine this "Twilight Zone" episode: Outside the house, families are playing active games, taking walks,

70

and attending the same social functions. Inside the home, parents and kids are playing board games and talking about the important and not–so–important moments of the day around the dinner table. I'm being tongue–in–cheek, but the point is that we need to make quality investments of time in the lives of our children.

Having a ritually scheduled child–parent event is a wonderful relationship builder. This can take the form of a weekly daddy–daughter date, a mother–son Saturday hike, or anything else you can imagine that interests the child. These relational rituals can also be smaller in scale, like reading a book together at bedtime when they're little, or cooking dinner together when they're older. The point of this is less about what we do, and more about the results of our doing it together. By investing quality time in our children's lives, we're building a firm foundation that we pray will stand strong in times of emotional distress.

Being There

Another way we can communicate to our children how much we value them is by being present at school functions and extracurricular activities. This is especially true, of course, when they're being singled out for any type of special recognition. Even if a child is getting nothing more than a participation award, it matters that we're there.

You may ask, "How can we attend our children's activities when our corps schedule is so hectic?" You'll never reach 100 percent. Calendar conflicts are unavoidable. However, we also control our calendar to a large extent—and I generally find that I can make time for those things I really want to make time for. If we can't be available to our children because of a schedule conflict,

> *Show them how important it is to you to be there for them. They will remember your presence for the rest of their lives. They will also remember your absence.*
>
> *—Armstrong and Morledge*
> *Help! I'm a Pastor*

we need to make sure they understand the unavoidable reason why. If you miss your child's choral concert at school to watch your favorite TV show, you've not only missed an opportunity for investment, but also made an emotional withdrawal from that child and—to return to the original metaphor—you may have done some damage to your familial foundation.

Our daughter, Brittany, is currently in college and living on her own. Now that Stacie and I are empty-nesters, we've replaced our daughter's presence at home with a 22-pound ginger cat. When we're going to be out of town for a few days, my wife will hide cat treats throughout the house. She read somewhere that this will keep the cat stimulated by engaging his hunting skills. My guess is that the next time we give the house a deep cleaning, we'll find hidden cat treats all over the place. I think the only thing the cat likes to hunt are places to sleep.

On the other hand, this general idea is a pretty good one when applied to our children. Placing notes and other

> *Our children hate our appointment.*
>
> *—an officer*

small surprises in school lunches or jacket pockets can be a great aid to building a positive and supportive relationship. Another good child–treat idea might be to make a point of remembering when your child is facing a big test at school and, at an appropriate moment, sending a simple text message to let him know that you care and are praying for him.

"In some ways a pastor's children grow up with ample reasons to resent, even distrust, the church. After all, is it not the church that always takes daddy and mommy away?" These challenging words appear in the book, *Help! I'm a Pastor,* by Richard Armstrong and Kirk Morledge. Since time allotment is the one area of pastoring our children over which we have the most control, it's incumbent on us to control it just as much as we can. Our children are not just little people who happen to live in our house. They're individual souls in need of our emotional and spiritual guidance and support.

Our Children and Our Ministry

Virtually every officer has at one time or another given testimony to having been called by God to serve Him in and through The Salvation Army. But what about our children? Does our calling mean that they are vicariously selected by God for this same ministry? Or does God retain the option to call them to a different ministry or life plan? Are our children helpless occupational participants in our calling? Different officers will answer these questions in different ways.

No matter how we view the role of our family members with regard to our ministry responsibilities, the reality is that some children thrive within their parents' ministry and are a great complement to it whereas others have great difficulty with the concept. Our children's struggle to identify who they are and how they fit into a ministry lifestyle can ultimately manifest in open rebellion against us, against the Church, and against God Himself.

Should your children be a component of your ministry? If so, to what degree? Your particular family dynamic, the Lord's leading, and your child's disposition and giftedness will provide the answer. Children who show enthusiasm for the ministry should be given opportunities to express themselves through this avenue of service to the Lord. But if your children don't want to be used in the corps, don't force the issue. Allow them to have some choice, especially as they grow older. What is our spiritual responsibility and ultimate goal for our families? To look good in front of our congregation and the administration? We have the higher calling of shepherding our children with love and spiritual discernment so that they will grow into adults who don't resent God and the Church, and who—when they are ready—will embrace Jesus in all His fullness as their personal Savior.

> *I need to know how to better manage my ministry and calling along with my marriage and raising of my children so that my pastoral ministry as an officer is not impeded.*
>
> *—an officer*

Regardless of whether our children are active participants in our work, they are likely to experience the pressure placed on most children whose parents are in full-time ministry: pressure to be perfect little examples of holiness. This pressure comes from people in the corps, from people in the community, from the administration—from pretty much everyone. H.B. London and Neil Wiseman contend that "66% of pastors and their families feel pressure to model the ideal family to their congregations and communities." This is, of course, an unrealistic burden for our children to carry. We need to let our children act like children—within reasonable limits. *Help! I'm a Pastor* includes these comments: "The pressures on pastors' children can be enormous. Without intending to, well–meaning church members and others in the community will hold them to a different standard." This holy squeezing can cause a child to burst into a spirited bout of rebellion. There's a reason why ministers' children often have a reputation for bad behavior.

Our children need us to be more than just corps officers. Here's an experiment to try with your family that may yield some startling results. The rules are simple: Invite your child to choose a fun word. From that point on, whenever your child says this word, everyone has to stop talking about the Army, or any other component of your ministry, and talk about something completely different. In our family the word was "star." To this day, any time our daughter says this word we immediately stop talking Army business and switch the conversation to something that is of interest to our whole family.

After our family instituted this rule, we were amazed to realize just how much we actually talked about Salvation Army "stuff." The second surprise was how difficult it was at first to fill a conversation without talking business. It took a lot of practice for us as a family to break out of the Army conversation bubble, but the benefits for our daughter have been wonderful. This word power invested her with a degree of control over the extent to which the Army had control over her. As Patrick Morley writes, "Growing up is harder on kids than adults. Let's give them the freedom to be kids."

The Weight of Words

"Sticks and stones may break my bones, but words will never hurt me." So my mother taught me when I came home from school crying because a classmate had publicly made fun of my curly hair. Love you, Mom, but you were wrong. Words matter a great deal. Words can be gloriously uplifting and affirming, or they can be used as a battering ram to destroy. Words are

> *Children are like wet cement. Whatever falls on them makes an impression.*
>
> *—Haim Ginott*
> *Between Parent and Child*

particularly powerful when they are spoken in the presence of children. It's important to keep in mind that our children don't possess the same level of mental processing that we have as adults. What we say to them is taken literally and taken seriously. When our children are very young, we are the source of all wisdom and truth. Even when they don't understand the context of what we are saying, and may misunderstand the content, they'll certainly copy the tone.

Consider for a moment how you talk about your ministry and about the wider Army in the presence of your children. If what our children hear are negative, degrading comments, what can we expect their thoughts and attitudes to be? Why would my child want to be a part of a corps that I continually speak of in a demeaning way?

There's not an officer who wouldn't change some aspect of the Army in some way. We all carry around a sack of our own opinions and perfect solutions to the problems of the day. But when it comes to our children's listening ears, not all of these thoughts need to be expressed—and if they are, we should take great care regarding how we express them. Consider for a moment what happens to our children's perceptions and attitudes if what they hear from us on a daily basis is a nonstop barrage of complaints and grievances about the Army. Then, when a move is announced and they are feeling tremendous pain and loss, how can we expect them to believe that the administration is God–led and that the transition is spiritually ordained?

Presenting our ministry to our children in a positive manner is especially important if we receive the fateful phone call and are personally dissatisfied with the destination. Our ministry lifestyle is already a heavy burden for our children to carry. So however we may feel about our new appointment, it's up to us to place our children's well–being above our own feelings and ambitions and to consider how our reaction to a transition will impact the way they handle this life–altering news.

Everyone around us is impacted by what we do and say—our children most of all. That means that we have a great opportunity to help our children prepare for the storms of life—by doing and saying the right thing. This is a crucial spiritual responsibility that I pray we all take very seriously. When we have children, our life ceases to be primarily about our own wants, needs, and desires. It's about what's best for them.

A PRAYER FOR A NEWBORN BABY

With joy and thanksgiving we come to Thee,
O Lord of Goodness and Love,
to praise Thee out of the fullness of our grateful hearts
that Thou hast gladdened our home and life
with this newborn babe.

Our joy is exceedingly great
as Thou hast preserved the mother,

who has gone down into the shadows
of death to bring forth this new life.

We know that this child is a gift
of Thy bountiful hand.

Grant us grace and wisdom to bring up
this precious soul in the knowledge and
understanding of Thy Word,
which makes all of us wise unto salvation.

Bless our child with a healthy body,
a clear mind, and a clean heart,
and preserve it to us
according to Thy good and gracious will.

Grant that our child may grow
in favor with Thee
and bring sunshine and joy into our hearts and our
home.

And now to Thee be praise, glory, thanksgiving
for this precious gift this day and forever;
through Jesus Christ,
who is the friend of children
and the Savior of all.

AMEN

Lutheran Book of Prayer (1951)

7

Weathering the Storm

*'Who among you will give your children
a stone when they ask for bread?*

*Or give them a snake
when they ask for fish?'*

Matthew 7:9–10 (CEB)

We sit staring at our phone early in the morning. We've been staring at it for a while now, waiting to see if it will ring. It's the day when the calls are made, the moves released. We've spent the entire weekend answering multiple questions from our corps people, our employees, and our peers: "Do you think you'll be moving?" Our pat answer has been something like, "I don't think so, but in the Army, you never know," or "God is in charge, so we'll see." Our peers' questions are the most incessant and sometimes the most irritating. Some of them view move time as a sport; they compete to see if they can predict who will be moving and where they will be sent. In our own minds, we've run through a list of places we think would be perfect for us and another list of appointments we would dread.

The clock finally hits the magic hour when we know the phone calls have started, and our nervous energy rises to a crescendo. We make sure for the hundredth time that morning that our phone ringer is on and the battery is charged. It would be terrible to be called but not be available because our phone battery had died. As we sit there in suspense, we find ourselves rooting internally: "Don't ring, don't ring, don't ring!" or "Come on, baby, and ring once for daddy!"

Suddenly the phone springs to life and the name on the screen is the divisional commander's. Instantly every muscle in our body contracts. For a split second, we can't decide how to answer. We wait until after the second ring because we don't want the DC to know we've been up for hours staring at the phone. Then we hit the answer button, and starting with a practiced greeting that comes out more fumbled and higher-pitched than we'd have liked it to, engage in a short conversation. After we hang up the phone, we sit still for a few minutes while we process what we've just heard.

We may or may not like the news concerning our new appointment, but whatever our personal feelings may be, what about our children? For the next six weeks our family will be living in the midst of an emotional storm. The list of tasks to be completed before physical move day is enormous, and the thought of actually being able to accomplish everything on that list seems impossible. How can we possibly take care of all of the community, corps, organizational, family, moving, and personal expectations in just six weeks? Every one of these areas of our life seems to be of the highest priority. It's enough to drive a person crazy. As our mind juggles all these issues, however, our first spiritual and emotional responsibility is for the well–being of our children.

Develop a Personal Plan

> *'Suppose one of you wants to build a tower. What is the first thing you will do? Won't you sit down and figure out how much it will cost and if you have enough money to pay for it?'* Luke 14:28–29 (CEV)

Jesus used a practical example from everyday life to make it clear that those who wanted to follow Him should first count the cost. But His brief parable illustrates another point as well—that many of life's most important endeavors require advance planning. And here's the intentional planning concept in a nutshell: Start from the end and work backwards. Our goal is that our children will be able to adjust to their new appointment environment with a minimal level of emotional distress and establish their new normal as quickly as possible. With this goal in mind, we carefully consider the necessary steps to take.

Once the proper foundation is laid, the first step in the process of "building that tower" is the completion of a personal plan tailor–made for the child who is to undergo the stresses and strains of a move. What does a personal plan look like? The following page contains a Personal Plan Template, showing the components that should be included.

Personal Plan Template

Reasons for each section

Basic Information
Name:_____

Age:_____   School grade:_____

Extracurricular activities:_____
_____

Personality type/tendencies:_____
_____

Rate: 1 (poor) – 10 (outstanding)
- School experience:_____
- Corps experience:_____
- Community experience:_____
- Friends experience:_____

What will my child miss the most?_____
_____

Who will my child miss the most?_____
_____

Identifying my child's
current 'normal'
(Get us thinking)

Transitional Six Weeks
Activities to do:_____
_____

People to interact with:_____
_____

Structured time for parental pastoring:_____
_____

Goodbye list:_____
_____

Closing and finishing
well in current
appointment

New Appointment Research
New school:_____
_____

New neighborhood:_____
_____

New community:_____
_____

Extracurricular activities:_____
_____

New corps:_____
_____

Preparing to work on
establishing
a new 'normal'

Plans for New Appointment
People to meet:_____
_____

Activities to engage in:_____
_____

Family events:_____
_____

Concrete plans for
new appointment

Whatever format you use in creating an individual plan, I strongly encourage you to write it out. This makes it "real," gives it substance—and helps you to remember what you have come up with. Once it's initially written out, it can act as a catalyst for new thoughts and ideas. You may end up deviating from the plan as events unfold; that's OK. Whatever you do, don't write a plan and then shelve it. That's like having a strategic plan created for your corps and then filing it away somewhere with no action taken. The impact of an unused plan is precisely zero; it might as well never have been created.

As shown in the template, a personal plan contains four sections. The first section involves thinking through who your child is as well as the general structure of your child's current normal. Understanding your child's likes and dislikes, disposition, and personality are foundational for developing a successful plan. For instance, if your child is an introvert, you will want to create opportunities for down time and self-reflection. It's great that everyone wants to give your family a farewell party, but remember that to an introvert, social situations such as this, during this time period especially, may simply exhaust precious emo-

I believe that there needs to be intentional work with officers' children.

—an officer

tional energy. As Marti Laney writes, "Introverts need time to cogitate without the pressure to 'do' something." The opposite is true for an extroverted child, who may need lots of social interaction in order to receive emotional energy. Many times, talking through issues and about how your child feels may be what is needed most to aid in mentally processing the transition.

The second section of the plan is focused on the six weeks of transitioning out of your current appointment. It revolves around activities that are geared toward the specific attributes of the individual child. These activities should be designed to allow your child to say goodbye to the people and places that have been "home" for a period of time and bring about some sort of closure.

The third and fourth sections of the plan call for the parent to conduct some research. Investigating the new appointment through the lens of what will best help your child in creating a new normal is critical. This will make it possible for you to do some advance planning. For example, if your child is like Piglet and loves to fly kites, try to have some kind of kite flying event arranged for when you arrive in the new community. These sections are discussed a bit later in this chapter, under the heading "Research the New Appointment."

Be the One to Break the News

There are many things about The Salvation Army that are truly amazing, like the way we can respond to disas-

> *It is important to have enough respect for your children and their feelings to make sure they learn about an upcoming move from you and your spouse in a private setting.*
>
> —*Lori Burgan*
> *Moving with Kids*

ters, or the way wearing our uniform opens so many doors in the community. But nothing in the Army is quite as impressive as our internal grapevine. The speed with which information about moves travels through the officer ranks is astound-

ing. Because of the efficiency of this communication system, there's a possibility that your child could learn about your imminent move before you've had a chance to break the news. Don't let this happen. It's important that you be the one to deliver the message so that you can properly measure your child's initial reactions and can provide immediate pastoral aid.

When we engage in the initial news–breaking conversation, we should be prepared for any reaction from our children, positive or negative. In addition to being ready to dispense happy, happy, joy, joy words, we should be prepared to deal with any negative emotional outbursts. Properly breaking the news of being moved and then providing pastoral comfort and leadership to our children are the very first steps toward establishing a new normal in the next appointment. Don't blow this moment. A misstep at this point can deepen your child's feeling of loss and lengthen the time of recovery required.

Listen, Listen, Listen

I was raised during a time when this old saying was still popular: "Children should be seen and not heard." In other words, when adults were talking, my duty as a child was to not disturb them. That was fine with me because I really didn't care about what they were saying. Unfortunately, a practical implication of this philosophy is that the problems children experience are not on the same level of importance as those faced by adults; so we say, "Just get over it." I hope we've progressed to a point where we understand that many of the problems we face as adults are rooted in childhood experience. If we can deal with issues of this kind when they are in seed form, when our children are struggling with them, we can eliminate much lifelong adult trauma.

The process of dealing with any problems that arise from the feelings of loss experienced during a move starts simply, with listening. When I first approached my daughter with the news that we were moving, in the incident I describe in the first chapter of this book, I came ready to convince her that this was going to be a great adventure. What I was not prepared to do was listen. Before I began my barrage of the great advantages to our move, I should have listened to her words and watched her initial reaction to the news.

Encourage and Protect Self-Expression

Different people express themselves in different ways. Some, particularly extroverts, prefer oral communication, whereas introverts may prefer something like journaling. Whatever means of personal expression is most comfortable for your child, facilitate and encourage it in an environment of absolute safety. After children have communicated their emotional thoughts and feelings, whether by speaking, writing, or in some artistic form, their expressions should never be used against them or mocked. Once there has been a betrayal of a child's emotional secrets, the likelihood of ever getting that child to fully open up again is severely curtailed.

If you have an orally oriented child, create opportunities away from other listening ears to sit and just talk, perhaps walking in a park or sitting in a coffee shop. During these moments of connection, it's very important that you not take offense to what your child is saying, even if the sentiments expressed hurt your feelings. Remember that we're the adults in such conversations, and once our children recognize that we are indeed safe to talk to, they're much more likely to continue to do that.

Helping your writing–oriented child with self–expression can begin with a visit to a bookstore to purchase a journal. Don't be cheap: buy whatever journal fits your child's personality the best. Then give

> *A personal journal is an ideal environment in which to 'become.' It is a perfect place for you to think, feel, discover, expand, remember, and dream.*
>
> — *Brad Wilcox*

your child the alone time required to use it. James Pennebaker of the University of Texas states, "Emotional upheavals touch every part of our lives.… Writing helps us focus and organize the experience.… Moving a troublesome situation from the background of your child's mind and onto center stage on the written page helps him process what happened and make sense of it all."

Make the Goodbyes Not So Bad

Drop a Mentos candy into a bottle of Coke and put the cap on. Pressure will build up inside the bottle until it explodes and messes up everything around it. The process of saying goodbye releases emotional energy that can reach an unhealthy level if kept bottled up. Children at every age form strong attachments to many aspects of their environment. Part of a healthy grieving process is the opportunity to actually say goodbye and bring closure to their connections with people and places that have acted as their security blankets and support mechanisms for many years. Creating a last visit event at one of your child's favorite places—a pizza parlor, school, store—whatever it might be—is one great way to provide such an opportunity. Wherever the event takes place and whatever form it takes, just try to make it as much fun as possible. A small child might draw pictures of places visited on the farewell tour to serve as positive reminders of this experience of closure.

When children are older, making the experience of saying goodbye to best friends positive and fun can prove to be a bit more challenging. Even so, it's important that your child have chances to say goodbye. Barbara Hey writes, "While goodbyes can be difficult, your child should be allowed to say farewell to her friends with a going-away party or a spe-

I think pastoral support for officers who are moved unexpectedly is very important. Especially when it involves disturbing our children's relationships.

—an officer

cial playdate." Saying goodbye to friends, even in the most entertaining environment, can become very emotional. Allow those emotions to be expressed and help your child to process through this ritual, which ideally can serve as a kind of internal cleansing. If the farewell tour is successful, your child will be better able to move forward and be prepared to establish new connections and friendships. If children are not afforded time and opportunity for goodbyes, they might try to hold on to past friends in an unhealthy manner, making it all the more difficult to form new connections.

When we receive our transfer news, it's our children who find themselves in the unenviable position of having to hurt their close friends by telling them of their imminent departure. It's already difficult enough for our children to enlighten their friends regarding the nature of The Salvation Army; the added burden of trying to explain a move across the country in just six weeks' time may be too much to handle. It can be tremendously helpful to our children if we aid them in conveying and explaining this news to their friends in a positive manner.

Empower Decision Making

The transfer of officers to a new appointment involves a lot of decisions made by a variety of people. Those with the least control over the situation are our children.

Feelings of powerlessness can cause some children to rebel or exhibit other types of negative behavior. Therefore, it's important for us as parents to find avenues for empowering our children. In Chapter 6, I suggested that a child be given a key word that would immediately shift the family conversation away from Army–related topics. During a move, there are a number of other possibilities for such empowerment.

The packing process presents several golden opportunities for giving a child a bit of authority. You can allow your child to decide what to pack first in which box or, in some cases, what's to be thrown away and what's to be kept. Let her write or draw on boxes of her own "stuff" to designate them as hers. The goal is to identify any opportunity possible for your child to feel some sense of control.

Pets can be a problem during this time, but they can also be a great asset. Putting your child in charge of helping a pet make the transition can also help the child in coping with change. Let your child make decisions about how the pet toys are going to be packed and participate in discussion of how the pet transfer is going to occur. After arriving in the new appointment, your child can help the pet become acclimated by finding new places to walk and play or can be involved in discovering new places to buy pet food. Seeing that Fido is making a successful transition can help your child do the same.

Research the New Appointment

The third section of the personal planning template calls for researching the new appointment to obtain information relevant to your child. The results of the research provide a basis for the concrete plans you will make to help your child make new connections and move toward a new normal—the fourth section of the plan.

Just as the goodbye tour included people and places, so does the welcome tour. Your research should include the community, relevant schools, the neighborhood, and extracurricular activities as well as the corps.

When our children are happy and progressing properly in their schooling we are more capable of fulfilling our ministry expectations.

—an officer

The research process presents another opportunity for you to empower your child—in helping to determine what areas to research and in what order. If your child is older, you might have him do much of the research and use the information he finds to help in educating you about the new community. For example, your child could research soccer leagues and where the fields are located. Then, together, you could make decisions on how to become involved and how to make contact with someone from a particular soccer association after you arrive.

Scheduling meetings with groups or individuals is also important to the process of transition. A word of caution, however: Don't take this step until your child is ready. Remember, you need to allow time for mourning and for saying goodbye. Prematurely forcing a child to look ahead to the new appointment can hang a negative cloud over the very things you're trying to use as positive inspiration. The best way to know if your child is ready to look ahead is to ask. Eventually your child's curiosity will come to the fore; then it will be time to future–cast and to make appointments with coaches, directors, teachers and others. Let your child set the pace of the interaction, even as you're conducting your research.

Make the Move an Adventure

The boxes have been packed, the quarters cleaned, and the brief written. The day has finally arrived when you pull away from your old normal and look forward to creating a new one. You're both exhausted and excited. You've left the old problems behind and haven't yet picked up the new ones. In a sense, this is a short sabbatical in which the family can bond together and have an adventure.

As much as you can, make the physical move fun. If there's a neat attraction along the way, one that your child will enjoy, take advantage of it. If there's a cool restaurant, stop and try something different. Whatever you can do to make it fun for your child, take the time and gather up your last reserves of energy to make it happen. Having fun can also include playing travel games, taking wild pictures, anything that will appeal to your children.

No matter how your child may be behaving or mis-behaving on any particular day during this six–week period, never forget the emotional storm that is raging and that you are the bulwark against that storm—always with the Lord's strong provision of help. If your child begins "acting up," the last thing you want to do is add your own negative energy to the situation. Patience is the key. And when your child's actions provide an op-portunity for positive reinforcement, take full advan-tage. A well–placed "atta boy" or "atta girl" can bolster your child's self–esteem and work to strengthen a tight relational bond.

ANGRY AT GOD

Me:
I told God I was angry.

I thought He'd be surprised.

I thought that I'd kept hostility
quite cleverly disguised.

God:

In telling Me the anger
you genuinely feel,
it loses power over you,
permitting you to heal.

Me:
I told God I was sorry
and He's forgiven me.

The truth that I was angry
has finally set me free.

Jessica Shaver

8

Recovery and Re-Establishment

Even children make themselves known by their acts,
by whether what they do is pure and right.

Proverbs 20:11 (NRSV)

One fine day Henny Penny was out under her favorite oak tree looking for food. As she pecked away, an acorn fell out of the tree and hit her on the head. Henny Penny immediately started running around, fully convinced that the sky was falling. Not stopping for a moment to think about what actually might have happened, she ran off down the road. The king had to be informed of this dire apocalyptic news!

As Henny Penny ran, she loudly squawked over and over—as only a chicken can—"The sky is falling! The sky is falling!" She soon came upon Goosey Loosey, Cocky Locky, Turkey Lurkey, and Ducky Lucky. One by one, each of them heard her cry and joined her in her frenzied state and in her important mission. They ran along together, feeding each other's sense of panic and determined to inform the king of the impending disaster: "The sky is falling! The sky is falling!"

The feathered friends turned a corner in the road, and there was Foxy Loxy! That stopped them in their tracks. Foxy Loxy wasn't about to be drawn into their emotional furor. With cool calculation and a few clever questions, he managed to trick the whole delegation into becoming his supper. The moral of the story: We can't make good rational decisions while we're experiencing irrational emotional tumult.

Arriving at a new appointment can certainly create an atmosphere of chaos. After all, everyone wants to meet the new officer to discuss issues concerning the appointment, even as our home is a pile of boxes and our children are in need of our emotional support and attention. All these ingredients mixed together can create a toxic brew for our family life. At this point, it helps to remember, "The race is not to the swift, nor the battle to the strong, but to the one who endures to the end." (Not exactly a quotation from the Bible; a kind of melding of parts of Ecclesiastes 9:11 and Matthew 24:13).

All of the many issues associated with a new appointment are not going to be addressed in the first month, It takes time, patience, and cool–headed wisdom to arrive at long–lasting solutions. However, these first days are very important to the psychological health and overall emotional recovery of our children.

Perhaps the most obvious thing you can do to help your child begin to create a new normal is to be available, both physically and emotionally. This is a time, during these first days, when children feel most alone and isolated. Our presence or absence can have a dramatic impact on them. However, when everyone is clamoring for our time, attention, and energy, how do we maintain focus on our children?

The only way to accomplish this goal is by setting clear, specific time priorities. For example, you might arrange a schedule in which meetings related

Did not have any children till well into my officership. It is hard finding a balance between the two.

—an officer

to your work are interspersed with meetings and events that are important to the life of your child. It's essential that you partner with your child in meeting teachers or directors of extracurricular activities and in discovering as many aspects as possible of the new environment.

The more supportive you are at this critical juncture, the sooner your child can recover emotionally and re–establish a new normal. And being supportive means, more than anything else, being present.

Allow Your Child to Grieve

As you walk in the door of your new appointment, there's an elephant in the room that must be faced and addressed. What was known has suddenly become unknown; the secure has overnight become insecure; the familiar is now unfamiliar. And grief didn't end with the goodbyes. The friends who would normally be there to help and support your child during this difficult time are far away and disconnected.

Not all children will grieve at the same level or in the same way. Discernment and wisdom are needed to properly facilitate emotional recovery. To properly understand what our children are feeling, we need to pay attention to how they're acting and what they're saying. Extreme behaviors that are out of character for a particular child are a clear signal of a need for our quality time and emotional attention.

When we were younger and didn't want to eat food we thought was yucky, someone would say: "Eat all your food. People in other countries are starving and would love to have your brussels sprouts." We're taking the same approach if we say things like, "Don't feel so bad; at least you have a home." or, "You need to get over your

*I need to learn
when to let go.*

— an officer

feelings. This move is what God wanted." The truth of statements such as these is irrelevant to a child who is grieving. What is needed instead is all the love and support we can give to them, minus the sermonizing and moral lesson training. There will be plenty of time for that once the initial crisis period is past.

The well–worn saying goes, "Time heals all wounds." If only that were true! The fact is that many adults live out their lives carrying deep wounds sustained during childhood. The reality is that actions heal wounds, not time. Think of it like this: You're walking through the woods and a huge thorn pierces your foot. You remove the thorn, but do you then sit down and wait for time to heal the wound? If you do, you'll slowly watch as the wound festers and causes ever–increasing levels of physical damage to your foot, your leg, and possibly your life. But let's say that your body fights off the infection and skin grows over the thorn. In that case you live on, but you'll have pain in your foot for the rest of your life that will not only be uncomfortable but will also affect how you walk. None of us would just sit and stare at our foot. We'd seek out medical help and take action that would bring healing.

We as parents are the first line of emotional assessment and healing for our children. If the wounds are greater than our ability to address them, we must seek out professional help. Our children are depending on us to do what is right and best for them. We must not let them down.

Set Up Your Child's Space—ASAP!

Toddler Rules

If I like it … it's Mine.

If it's in my hand … it's Mine.

If it looks like mine … it's Mine.

If I think it's mine … it's Mine.

Everything else … it's Mine.

Anonymous

When our children are toddlers, the "everything is mine" aspect of their behavior is cute. Older children have a more limited and more realistic view of what is theirs to rule over. Their kingdom, at best, generally consists of one room: their bedroom. This space is sacrosanct because it's the one place where the child can be in charge. It's also the one space for escape from the pressures and tensions of life and for contem-

There needs to be genuine concern for teens and young adult children, and support for inherited problems when moving to new appointments.

—an officer

plation and self–reflection. Because of its importance in providing emotional stability as well as personal security and control, your child's room should take a high priority when you're establishing the new family nest.

In setting up your child's room, don't just unpack boxes. Use this as an opportunity for your child to establish a sense of personal space. One of the best ways of accomplishing this is by simply buying a can of paint, two paint brushes or rollers, and painter's tape. With these items, you can help your child create a place of solace and proprietorship. Painting the room together also provides an opportunity for relational bonding and talking about how both of you are feeling. The faster and better this new safe haven is established, the quicker your child can move on with the process of establishing a new normal in this new place.

If you have more than one child, it may be that two or

more of your children share a room. If that's the case, try to make one part of that room—or another room in the house—a special "own place" for each of the children.

Create New Traditions with Your Child

Children, especially those who are naturally introverted, thrive on daily routines. During a time of transition such as a move, loss of predictable family activities contributes to the feelings of grief they're experiencing. To facilitate the establishing of a new normal, it's important to construct new family patterns.

If possible, renew traditions from the previous appointment, making adjustments as necessary. For instance, if your family has always enjoyed going out for a Saturday morning breakfast extravaganza, quickly identify a new special restaurant and keep the rhythm in place. If in your previous appointment you had a daddy–daughter bowling night, find a bowling alley in your new community and re–establish that routine—even if the program schedule in your new corps requires that you move it to another night of the week.

If it's not possible to replicate a fun activity that was a regular part of your family routine in the old appointment, create a new tradition with a new event. These can be simple, like how we get the mail or how we're going to walk the dog. Just make sure the activity is fun—so that your child will look forward to it and not think of it as a task that must be done. And invite your child's input. For example, if you establish a Friday night mother–son ice cream outing, allow your child to have some say regarding which ice cream place is chosen. The point of the activity is not the ice cream; it's the taking of another step toward a new normal.

Spend Time with Your Child

In addition to new family routines, spontaneous bouts of fun family adventures are also a good means of relieving emotional tensions and strengthening family bonds. Another benefit of these unplanned outings is that they can help you and your child to investigate and learn more about your new environment. Some spur–of–the–moment adventures can be easy to assemble, such as packing a lunch and walking to the local park for a picnic. As you're walking, keep an eye out for other families who appear to be moving into the neighborhood so you can attempt to interact with them. If one of those families has a child the same age as yours, you've hit the jackpot. How great would it be if your child entered his new school on the first day and actually knew another child!

Some fun activities may cost a little money, but if they bring a bit of emotional relief to your child and draw the family closer together, they're absolutely worth it. These might include attending a sporting event, a concert, or a community fair. Other ideas can also help you and your child learn about specific aspects of your new community. For example, go around town for a couple of weeks finding every place that makes cupcakes. Then decide together which one of these places makes the best ones, the prettiest ones, or maybe something random like the fluffiest ones. If your child is a reader, check out every bookstore in town to decide which one has the most books—or which has the most helpful staff.

Help Your Child Find New Friends

A rabbit named Oscar moves into a new town and wants to make new friends. At first Oscar doesn't join in playing with others because he's carrying around a critical attitude. However, he soon comes to the realization that unless he joins in and plays well with others, he'll end up with no friends at all. That's the story related by Rob Lewis in his children's picture book, *Friends*. Oscar's experience applies to all of us; if we sit in our room and wait for friends to show up at our door, we'll probably be sitting there alone for a very long time. That doesn't mean that you should force your child into extracurricular events and activities. But you should stand ready to facilitate and provide opportunities for peer interaction.

The place to begin is with what your child enjoys.

If your child is a musician, then find openings for musical expression. If there's no community children's symphony or other group, look into places that provide music lessons. You might strike up friendships with other parents during your child's lesson. Then, as appropriate, look for opportunities to translate your parental conversations into interaction between your child and other children who enjoy playing. Be creative in your thinking. If you facilitate the building of an interactive platform, your child will likely take the next step and create their own peer friendships.

Facilitate Your Child's Entry into School

You might think of your child as standing on a three–legged stool that represents adaptation to the realities of your new appointment. The sturdiness of that stool represents how quickly that adaptation proceeds and how well it succeeds. The three legs of the stool are your child's initial experiences in school, the corps, and extracurricular activities. The combination of these three will go a long way in determining your child's overall attitude toward the appointment. Of the three, entering a new school is probably the most critical. It's very important that you do everything you can to help your child navigate this transition.

Setting the stage for a successful school change

starts before you reach the new appointment. Hopefully, by the time you move in, you have already fully investigated your child's new school and possibly already reached out to set up a pre–opening tour with an administrator. If your child can visit the school beforehand and learn the overall layout, it will help to reduce some of the anxiety associated with the impending FIRST DAY. If a visit with at least one of your child's teachers can be arranged before school starts, that's golden. Your goal is to have your child as familiar and comfortable as possible with the new school and teachers before starting to navigate the even scarier waters represented by the other students.

> *A successful transition to a new school is one of the most important parts of a child's adjustments to a new home.*
>
> —*Lori Burgan*
> *Moving with Kids*

Another idea you might consider, depending on your child's age and disposition, is becoming a school volunteer. Even if you can't volunteer on a regular basis because of your schedule, you can still offer your services for class field trips or help from time to time with a school club that intersects with your child's interests. This affords additional interactions with teachers and administrators and may also give you opportunitiess to monitor your child's progress in peer integration.

Have a Positive Attitude and a Long–Term View

You have just moved your child into a new environ-ment, inducing an elevated level of anxiety. Because your child doesn't have a new peer social foundation established as yet, she is looking to you for interactive stability and support. Consider, then, how your child would interpret and mentally process a negative attitude emanating from you. You may be disappointed, sad, or even angry about your new appointment, but it's detri-mental to your child to place your emotional burdens on her. After all, if you believe that the Lord has called you to be an officer in the service of His Kingdom, you need to act like that's what you believe.

It's also important that you approach every appoint-ment with a long–term view. How can your child pos-sibly engage in meaningful peer relationships if you are constantly expressing the desire or belief that the new ap-pointment is only temporary? After your child has moved out of the nest, you can seek to move every six months if that's what you want. But until then, your concern should be your child's stability and sense of belonging. Believe me, your child knows that your next move could come at any time; no reminders of that are needed, nor are longings to move on because of career aspirations.

Watch for Signs of Depression

In the days when children still spent time outside playing, one popular game was Kick the Can. The premise and rules of the game were simple: Kick the can from point A to point B, then do it again, and again, and again, right down the street. The game has become a metaphor for procrastinating, for putting off till tomorrow what we could do today. Procrastination may be OK when it comes to things like washing the dishes or taking out the trash, but not when it comes to the mental health of our children. Internal wounds are like external ones; the longer they're left untreated, the deeper the scars, the longer the time it takes for them to heal, and potentially the more dramatic the procedure required to ultimately address them.

So what should you do if your child is exhibiting signs of aggression, depression, or anxiety that don't seem to be improving?

- Don't panic or overreact.

  The last thing you want to do is to elevate the stress and anxiety your child is already dealing with. Try to be very calm and methodical in how you talk about what your child is feeling. Approach your child as an advocate, not as an interrogator demanding answers.

- Try to identify the specific sources of the anxiety.

  There might be a single reason for your child's inability to properly adjust that you can help with. For instance, if you learn that your child is feeling depressed because of a bully at school, you can address this single issue in an appropriate way.

- Don't be afraid to say no on behalf of your child.

  You naturally want your child to become integrated into the new environment as quickly as possible. However, if your child is feeling overwhelmed by all the newness, then leap into the breach and say no. Here's an example: You've already had your welcome Sunday, but the Advisory Board wants to have an evening community meet–and–greet for you and your family; however, your child is emotionally not up for the event. If at all possible, don't force your child to attend or induce a sense of shame or guilt for not being there.

- If needed, seek professional help.

  If you discern that your child's emotional state is not

improving and that it's beyond your capacity to help any more than you already have, PLEASE REACH OUT FOR PROFESSIONAL HELP. It could be that a single professional assessment would make a world of difference in your child's attitude and in the strategies you need to employ as a family.

> *Please continue to make available counseling services through Christian professional counselors.*
>
> *—an officer*

In Aesop's fable of "The Tortoise and the Hare," the two protagonists agree to a race. The hare approaches the challenge with arrogance and takes off at top speed ... until he sits down for a rest. The tortoise sets a slow but steady and unchanging pace. The result is that against all odds, the tortoise wins. Thus the maxim: "Slow and steady wins the race."

You've just moved. Your child is emotionally churned up and in need of your help, support, and guidance (even if he's older and acts as though he doesn't). Your approach should be slow and steady, not marked by fits of doing too much and then not enough. Don't worry about winning races. Your child is your spiritual, emotional, and physical responsibility. Make that a priority and stick with it.

A MOTHER'S PRAYER

Dear Lord,
It's such a hectic day,
with little time to stop and pray.
For life's been anything but calm,
since you called me to be a mom—
running errands, matching socks,
building dreams with stacking blocks.
Cooking, cleaning and finding shoes,
and other things that children lose.
Fitting lids on bottled bugs,
wiping tears and giving hugs.
A stack of last week's mail to read—
where's the quiet time I need?
Yet, when I steal a moment, Lord,
at the sink or ironing board,
to ask the blessing of your grace,
I see then, in my little one's face,
that you have blessed me all the while.
And I stoop to kiss that precious smile.

anonymous

9

Inside Out:
A Visual Aid

Parents, don't be hard on your children.

Ephesians 6:4 (CEV)

Our daughter was home for a short visit during a break from college when we as a family decided to go out one evening to do something fun and different. I was pressing for us to go see a drive–in movie as we hadn't been to one in decades. The movie that night was a new animated feature called *Inside Out*. Our plan was to enjoy the evening air, laugh together, eat popcorn, and be mildly entertained. So we parked the minivan on that crazy little incline, opened the back hatch of the vehicle, unfolded our chairs, bought lots of unhealthy food at very high prices, and looked forward to a fun night. Well … this was one of those "best–laid plans" that didn't turn out quite as expected. Instead of a pleasant time of shared laughter and family inside jokes, the night became a deeply moving event.

What we didn't know beforehand was that the animated movie we were about to see would end up touching a significant familial nerve. Certainly there was some giggling, but as the story unfolded, we were reminded of our own past struggles. Don't let me scare you away from this movie: I think every officer parent and child should experience it. Many adult officers' children have told me how wonderfully it encapsulates their own life experiences.

Inside Out is the story of an 11–year–old girl, Riley, who is moving with her mother and father from Minnesota to San Francisco because of a job advancement opportunity for the dad. In the beginning stages of the story, everything seems to be going well, with Riley embracing the idea of relocating. The car ride to San Francisco is exciting, filled with visions of how great things are going to be in their posh new house near the Golden Gate Bridge. However, when they arrive, Riley quickly discovers that reality isn't quite living up to the mental picture she has created in her mind. Feelings of disappointment start to overtake her as she sees the scary–looking empty house and goes into her dusty bedroom—where she finds a dead mouse. As the days pass, the sources of personal disappointment increase and cut across every aspect of Riley's life. During Riley's downward emotional slide, we watch her experience profound disconnection, disappointment, and loneliness.

Riley's Transition Cycle

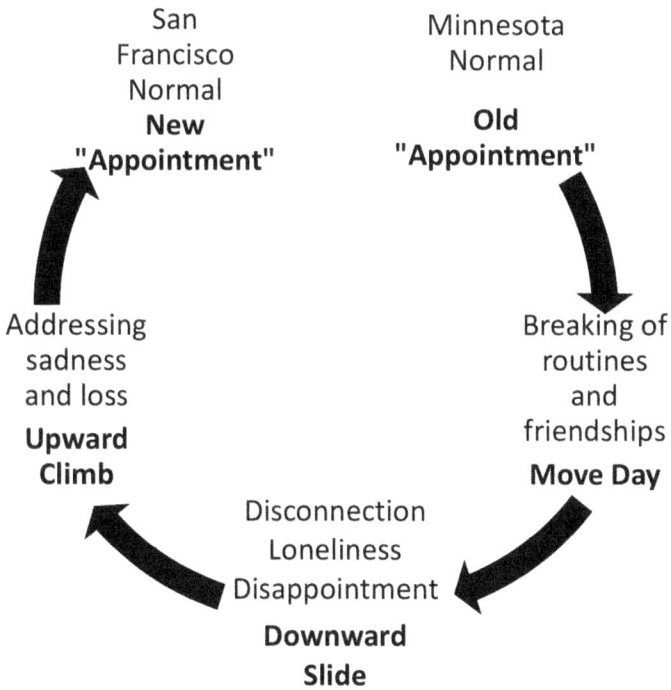

San
Francisco
Normal
New
"Appointment"

Minnesota
Normal
Old
"Appointment"

Addressing
sadness
and loss
Upward
Climb

Breaking of
routines
and
friendships
Move Day

Disconnection
Loneliness
Disappointment
Downward
Slide

The Downward Slide

Dad: *Riley, I do not like this new attitude.*

Riley*:*   *What is your problem, just leave me alone!*

Dad: *I don't know where this disrespectful attitude came from.*

Riley: *Yeah well......... Just shut up!*

Dad: *That's it! Go to your room!*

Disconnection

While living in Minnesota, Riley had felt a deep sense of connectedness with her friends, school, and hockey team, as well as with her parents. She also enjoyed a connection with a familiar physical environment—her home and her bedroom, the nearby ice–skating lake and local pizzeria. As the early scenes of the movie unfold, Riley's sense of belonging is slowly stripped away, piece by piece, until she feels like there's nothing left. Everything she recognizes as her normal disappears. In addition to the disconnect from her friends, life routines, and physical environment, Riley is experiencing extreme dislocation from her chief support network, her immediate family. Her dad has a new job that he wants to learn quickly and be good at, so that occupies his time—time that he used to set aside for daddy–daughter interaction. Riley's mother is a bit more conscious of the fact that her daughter is suffering, but she keeps trying to make everything better by be-

> *We are all things to all people. Family life gets put on hold a lot. The children act out and we are so stressed from what we do, they suffer.*
>
> —*an officer*

ing "positive." This leaves no room for Riley to express her feelings, which serves to increase the disconnection and isolation she is experiencing.

Children and adults alike are largely defined by their immediate environment, including their social connections, normal routines, and physical surroundings. When you or I interact with an unfamiliar officer, one of the first questions we ask is, "Where are you stationed?" This is followed by a set of questions concerning familial status. As we continue to interact, there invariably comes a moment when the family pictures begin to be passed around with a short narrative highlighting each child's very best accomplishments and qualities. In the case of Stacie and me, as empty nesters with no grandchildren, our cat is beginning to show up in those family pictures as well.

The questions that help define who a child is take similar form: "What school do you go to?" "What do you do for fun?" "What is your house like?" When officers are transferred to a new appointment, their child's connections are stripped away. The answers to those defining questions are centered on the previous appointment, bringing to the fore all that has been lost. So how can our children define themselves during those pivotal first days?

Disappointment

One of the mistakes my wife and I made in trying to mitigate our own daughter's hurt when we moved during her middle school years was to try to oversell the glories of the place we were moving to. This seemed like a good strategy at the time of packing the boxes, but overselling can actually backfire when the boxes are being unpacked.

In the movie, Riley's expectations are built up tremendously—so much so that no reality could ever measure up to what she imagines. From the moment she sees San Francisco through the car window, her slide into ever–deepening levels of disappointment begins. It turns out that the Golden Gate Bridge isn't gold after all.

> *Depression begins with disappointment. When disappointment festers in our soul, it leads to discouragement.*
>
> —Joyce Meyer

In addition to the new house and her bedroom, Riley's disappointments—piling up, one on top of the other—include embarrassment at school, loss of regular routines, loss of the moving truck with her personal items, and failure at hockey tryouts. Even the local pizzeria makes only broccoli pizza! Each officer's child who is forced to move will have a different list of disappointments, but every child will be impacted by them. To oversell a new community is setting a child up for future disappointments.

Loneliness

Loneliness is difficult for adults to deal with. Imagine what it can be like for a child. Unfortunately, loneliness tends to be a natural part of the moving cycle as a child is disconnected from one normal and searching desperately to re–establish a new normal. Riley experiences a deep sense of loneliness because of her loss of connectedness to her school friends, her hockey team, and her parents. The emotional pain is magnified by the fact that all of these losses occur simultaneously at a time when she is in most need of support.

> *The loneliest moment in someone's life is when they are watching their whole world fall apart, and all they can do is stare blankly.*
>
> *—F. Scott Fitzgerald*
> *The Great Gatsby*

The disconnection from her parents is the final straw for Riley. Her father and mother are deeply involved in their own life transitions and don't fully recognize the difficulties and relational disruptions Riley is going through. They also don't realize that Riley desperately needs connectedness with her parents, much more so than she did in Minnesota. This need becomes even more acute when Riley's closest friend from Minnesota innocently indicates that she is moving on, bonding with other friends.

When we as officers move into a new appointment, it's easy to recognize the programmatic, financial, property and corps issues that need to be addressed in a timely manner. But it's critical that we make time to consider the loss of a peer support structure and the social relationship void that our children may be experiencing.

The Upward Climb

Riley: *I … I know you don't want me to, but … I miss home, I miss Minnesota. You need me to be happy, but I want my old friends, and my hockey team. I wanna go home. Please don't be mad.*

[Riley's mother and father stare sadly at their daughter]

Mom: *Oh, sweetie …*

Dad: *We're not mad. You know what? I miss Minnesota too. I miss the woods where we took hikes.*

Mom: *And the backyard where we used to play.*

Dad: *Spring Lake, where you used to skate.*

[Riley breaks down in tears]

Dad: *Come here.*

[Riley, her mother, and her father all embrace in a group hug]

With a sense of hopelessness engulfing her, Riley reaches a point of full crisis and runs away from home to catch a bus to Minnesota. In her mind, everything will be better if she can only get back to where she last was happy and secure. She is desperately trying to find her past normal. This futile effort is abandoned only when the appeals to, "Be happy, everything will be fine," cease and Riley allows herself to feel sadness and grief. Then she and her parents can finally mourn the loss of what had been their reality and start to embrace what can be.

New Normal

Throughout the animated movie, various emotions—Anger, Joy, Sadness, for example—have become characters in Riley's head. Once the crisis of the move has passed, Joy is able to assure the other characters that they can enjoy the new direction Riley's life has taken.

> Joy: *We've been through a lot lately, that's for sure, but we still love our girl. She has great new friends, a great new house … things couldn't be better! After all, Riley's 12 now, what could happen …*

THE END

By the end of the movie, Riley is busy re–establishing her new normal. In order to be emotionally free to do this, she has to go through the steps of facing the losses she has experienced, mourning those losses, and bringing closure to what had been her reality in Minnesota. How quickly and effectively any child develops a new normal in a new appointment also depends on how well these same steps are addressed. As parents, we can't force our children to transition well, but we can be intentional in doing everything within our power to help facilitate their emotional recovery.

I AM MOVING: A CHILD'S PRAYER

God, please help me with the move,

so far away from here.

Help me make some new friends

that are just like the old.

Help me to get adjusted and to have fun again.

Please, be with me.

Loyola Kids Book of Everyday Prayers

An Open Letter from an Officer's Child

By Brittany McWilliams

Parents are traditionally charged with the responsibility to create a stable environment for their children to grow up in. To know stability when you're young is to trust life later on, regardless of what gets thrown at you; to know instability is to face a very challenging period of being unable to trust all that is around you. I have always felt that I fell into the second category: childhood instability. Not because my parents lacked anything, but rather because my life and everything I built was consistently threatened with ruin. When you are constantly faced with the threat of being uprooted, you become unable to ever truly invest in where you are. You never really have a place where you belong, and there is a wall between you and everything around you, but you seem to be the only one who knows it's there.

In the very recent past, I have been forced to come to terms with this issue of instability. I have been an officer's kid all my life. I have known nothing else. When I learned that normal people move with their own furniture and washing machines, I was flabbergasted. I have worn the uniform, signed the pledges, gone on the mission trips, and been to the summer camps. I have attempted to learn brass instruments and performed more timbrel drills than I can count. I have spent every year of my life anxiously waiting to find out if that would be the year I would have to move or not. I remember the spring mornings when my parents would keep me home from school because they knew we would be getting a call, and I remember the times they swore we wouldn't, but we still did. I know the way your mom broaches the subject with you when she picks you up from school that afternoon, and I know the promises your dad makes to you about taking you to Disney World to make up for it.

I've also heard the justifications, and I've been told to buck up and move on. I have been through the confusion, anger, and even hatred. At least for me, the most common justifications for moving I was given had to do with it being God's purpose and with considering the positive sides of it. Certainly those concepts have their place, but they don't really have a place in the mind of a 12-year-old who has just been told she will have to leave everything behind. Telling a child that it's God's purpose for her is a tricky business, because you are automatically associating the pain, confusion, and grief of that situation with God's will. In reality, the burden is the parents' choice, but the children have to bear so much of it. It's like taxing your colony without giving them representation in Parliament: it just isn't fair. To deny that this is the truth is not helpful.

It's also important to remember that any positives that come from moving are not grounds to dismiss the negatives. There is good and bad in any situation, and they are not mutually exclusive. I would not be where I am today in life had I not grown up the way I did, but that in no way means I cannot grieve for the loss and pain I felt as a child.

Being allowed to grieve is so important. In any major life change, this is important. Far too often, we feel that we must power through and be OK, but that is false. It is unhealthy to not give ourselves space to be angry, hurt, upset, or whatever it is we may feel. As an adult, you get to think that through for yourself, but as a child, you need to be led through that kind of thinking. Going through a major transition during your childhood years is considerably more traumatic than going through it later on in life. Children don't have the coping mechanisms for it, and in the case of officers' kids, they also may not have a history of stability that would indicate to them that the transition will ultimately be OK. Having that difficulty acknowledged is, I think, the most important first step to take. Acknowledging and accepting the difficulty of a move in no way degrades the fact that it may be God's purpose, but it seems, to me at least, that many ministers tend to view it that way. Creating a safe space for a child to process big ideas and heavy emotions is, I think, actually a better way to promote the idea of God's love.

When I began to really delve into the issues I had developed over the years, I began to realize that two of my biggest problems were that I was lonely and that I didn't feel that I belonged anywhere. I didn't grow up anywhere in particular, and now when people ask me where I'm from, I answer with "Boston," a place where I never spent any childhood years. But belonging and loneliness are a lot more complicated than not having a physically steady home. They relate back to this ominous cloud you are forced to live under all your life. I feel that I spent most of my life living only halfway. I was like a runner waiting on the starting blocks. Because of this, I became very good at only half–engaging with the world around me. I had strong relationships that I would manipulate to make sure that I could always leave them. I would never want to keep my room the same way for more than a few months at a time. I never wanted to feel like anywhere was home, or like anything was comfortable.

Of course, because I was young, I didn't understand my own feelings, and in fact, I interpreted them in the opposite way. It seemed to me that I had no home, that no relationship could ever last, and that I would never feel comfortable. I felt that those were things that were being done to me or that were innately a part of me. It felt like it was some kind of shortcoming I had that kept the world so distant from me. I subconsciously learned to sabotage any relationship that got too serious. I would ruin friendships, and I would break down my relationships with boyfriends. I thought I was damaged, and I would even tell people I started getting close to that I should come with a warning label because I knew I would inevitably mess it up.

I am now almost 22 years old, I have moved away from home, and I get to choose for myself whether or not I move again. I have given myself the grace to deal with the pain I didn't deal with when I was younger, and I have come to a place of stability. Ironically, I'm the one in my family creating residential stability, not my parents. I write all this not to blame anyone or to say that moving a kid around is something that shouldn't be done. I write here about the pain I have struggled with through my life so that I can hopefully shed some light on what it feels like for those of you who don't know. Recognizing and experiencing our hurting is not an unnatural or bad thing. Grieving is healthy. Allowing yourself to be angry is important, because if you bury it, it will only bubble up again in a much nastier form than before. To deny yourself or anyone else the right to this emotional process is incredibly unhelpful.

I'm not a parent, but I can imagine that as one, you would want to do whatever you can to minimize the hurt your child feels when you announce a move. I can see how covering it up with talk of the positives or explaining it away by saying it's God's doing can seem like good solutions. Maybe it's even that as a parent, you have no idea how to justify it to yourself, so how could you explain it to your child? I don't know, but whatever the case is, I think justification and trying to Band–Aid the pain is impossible and unhelpful. Moving is not easy; never pretend that it is. Don't diminish the pain your child feels by immediately throwing fanciful ideas on top of it, or push the thought that because it's God's will, everything's OK. If you're going to choose a life of residential instability for yourself, make sure you have the resources to work through it with your children too.

Enough time has passed by this point in my life to make all of this feel very distant. I get to watch my parents gossip about whether they're going to move or not, and I don't really have to care about it. I have created a stability inside myself. It took a long time to build, and I went through a lot of pain before I got there. Even so, I would not change the experience for anything. My life has led me to places I never would have expected, and I have seen my parents grow through all of it as well. Life is too short to waste with anger and bitterness in your heart. Deal with it together as a family. Be with each other, support each other, and respect what your family is feeling. Moving is a difficult process, but I think it is one where love and grace can be employed in a manner that would certainly serve God's will.

10

Out of Our House But Not Out of Our Hearts

'And the son said to him, "Father, I have sinned against heaven and before you.

I am no longer worthy to be called your son."

But the father said to his servants, "Bring quickly the best robe, and put it on him, and put a ring on his hand, and shoes on his feet.

And bring the fattened calf and kill it, and let us eat and celebrate.

For this my son of mine was dead, and is alive again; he was lost, and is found." '

Luke 15:21–24 (ESV)

The Greek storyteller Aesop, writing in the 6th century B.C., taught practical wisdom through fables, short stories populated mostly by animals. One of his fables is "The Dog and His Bone." The story goes like this:

> A dog, crossing a bridge over a stream with a bone in his mouth, saw his reflection in the water and thought it was another dog much bigger than himself with a bone twice the size of his. He immediately dropped his bone and sprang at the dog in the stream to get the larger bone. He lost both, of course: the bone he grasped at in the water, because it was only a reflection, and his own bone, because the stream swept it away.

The moral of the story is that we, as human beings, can allow the passion of a moment to overwhelm our reason, the results of which may be catastrophic.

Aesop's story is a good metaphor for what sometimes happens to our adult children. They can be rolling along wonderfully through life when all of a sudden, they make a wrong choice that has a negative impact on the rest of their lives. Or perhaps it's not a single event, but a slow decline made up of multiple bad decisions—each one apparently minor in itself—that cumulatively result in a life being "off the rails." Regardless of how

Out of Our House But Not Out of Our Hearts

our adult children end up in difficult situations, we as parents can be at a loss as to how to help them.

For many of us, the most difficult parenting years are those after our children have left the nest. We still carry the burdens of worry, but now we are unable to exercise any control.

> *We have a divorced child who is not making good decisions. We struggle with our ongoing involvement in issues relating to this.*
>
> *—an officer*

Nothing can tear out our hearts more completely than watching from afar as our adult children struggle while we have no real power to fix things. When life is battering our children, even if they've created their own messes, we want to roll them up in a blanket on our lap and once again take care of all their boo–boos.

The issues our adult children face may range from deciding where to live or what job to take all the way to alcoholism, drug abuse, divorce, single parenting, chronic joblessness, chronic homelessness, mental illness, depression, eating disorders, legal troubles, arrests, financial ruin, family estrangement, ungodly living, and so on and on. What can we do if we see our children floundering?

139

'Pull Up Your Socks!'

I learned this expression from my very Irish mother. It means to get over our own sense of self–pity, self–loathing, and hopelessness and resolve to attack an issue, no matter what the obstacles may be. Dr. Jane writes,

> A central aspect of parents' identity is evaluating how our children have turned out; that is, what kind of adults they have become. The lives of our grown children constitute an important lens through which we judge ourselves and our accomplishments; it is through reconsidering their adult successes and failures that we seek, retroactively, to validate the kinds of parents we were and the responsible caring we provided.

It's easy for us as parents to dissolve into a heap of despair because we believe that our own success or failure in life is measured by our children's performance. This belief in itself can act as a hindrance to our being able to effectively help our children.

Whether we realize it or not, our sense of disappointment in our struggling children can be communicated to them through our words, actions, and body language. If our children sense a high level of parental disappointment, that can drive them further toward a negative self–image and/or create a greater gap in the parent–child relationship. Therefore, before we can become a good resource and

> *My oldest son is going down the wrong path and it weighs on me.*
>
> —an officer

positive help to our children, we have to pull up our socks and overcome our own sense of guilt and shame. The key is to realize that it's not about how I feel or how I fear others will judge me. It's about what my child needs from me today.

As we watch our adult children struggle with any problem, a variety of negative thoughts, emotions, and debilitating questions may overtake us: "What did I do wrong?" "What more should I have done?" "Did I give too much love, or not enough?" "Did I exercise too much control, or not enough?" For us as Salvation Army officers, of course, there's also: "How much has my child been harmed by all those times we moved from one appointment to another?" These "shoulda coulda woulda" questions can go on endlessly if we allow them to. However, if our goal is to help our children overcome their struggles and be successful, we have to move past our own self–abuse and self–pity and figure out what we can do for them now. The real question we need to ask ourselves is: "What are the BEST PRACTICES, in relation to my actions and words, that I can contribute today in order to produce the GREATEST BENEFITS for tomorrow for my adult children and myself?"

Adopt the Proper Perspective

Familial relationships can become murky due to our closeness to the situation. It's the old problem of "not seeing the forest for the trees." We may continue to view our adult children as our little munchkins. And it can be hard to discern the roots of our children's struggles because of our own wagonload of emotional baggage and unrealistic expectations.

As we're observing and assessing our adult children's needs, there are two key concepts that are important to keep in mind. First, our expectations for our children may not be the same expectations they have for themselves. As we watch our children grow, we construct grand plans in our minds for who and what they'll be one day. We see them through the lens of our own definitions of future glory. For instance, when a child achieves good grades in school, we imagine him becoming a high-level professional; when a child achieves success in sports, we imagine her becoming a great athlete. You get the picture. In reality, no child is likely to be or do what we envision, in choice of career or anything else. So the success or failure of our adult children should not be measured by how close they have come to our ideal for them, but by whether they can live a happy, fulfilled life.

I have married children with financial and marital problems who look to us for help.

—an officer

The second key thought to keep in mind is that the condition or position of our adult children's lives is not our responsibility. Our job is to do all we can to provide the best opportunity for them to be happy. When dealing with adult children, force, anger, threats, and chastisements are—to say the least—not the best tools to use. If your young child is throwing a temper tantrum in a store, you can forcibly pick the child up and leave the premises. As adults, our children will generally respond negatively to any attempt on our part to use force. Instead, we need to be available to them, loving, steady in our resolve, and wise in evaluating their needs—then decide what help we can realistically provide.

Keep Open the Door of Professional Help

Time–traveling through the years of our children's development, from changing diapers to navigating ever–more–complex schooling issues, eventually we get to watch with pride as our babies become independent young men and women. At each of these various life stages, we as parents stand in awe of our child's new abilities even as we're saddened over what has been lost from the previous stage. In our household, Stacie's and mine, we still long for the days when our little one would come home from preschool singing the "Baby Bumblebee" song:

> *I'm bringing home a baby bumblebee,*
> *Won't my mommy be so proud of me,*
> *I'm bringing home a baby bumble bee,*
> *Ouch! It stung me!*

As little Brittany shouted "Ouch," her hands would fly open and we would beg her to do it again.

As we travel this developmental road with our children, we can become convinced that we always know what's best for them. However, this simply may not be the case. We may be fantastic parents who have never spoken an unwise word, yet our children may be more willing to open up and receive advice from someone else, particularly someone who seems safe and is professionally trained. Counselors and psychiatrists

> *Help for my children who are living non-Christian lives. A child who is divorced with children.*
>
> *—an officer*

are detached and free of the emotional baggage that distorts our own interactions with our children. Whenever possible, Christian counselors are preferred, as they understand and appreciate the spiritual aspects of the child's personality and problems and are equipped with spiritual resources to aid in the healing process.

How do we keep the door of help open to our struggling adult children? Our own attitude in this area will have tremendous impact. If we have expressed ourselves in a negative or mocking way with regard to people who seek professional help, we may have slammed the door shut. Our attitude will affect how willing our adult children are to receive such help and how open they will be during assessment and counseling. We should not look upon a resort to professional intervention as a stain on our parenting history or our faith. Trained practitioners are gifts God has provided to aid in healing our bodies and our minds. It's up to us to take advantage of these gifts.

Another way in which we can be helpful in facilitating professional support for our children is by providing some level of financial backing. What is it worth to us to see our adult child healthy and whole? It can't be measured.

Evaluate Your Behavior

How can we as parents possibly close any door to our children when they are struggling or in pain? In response to that question, consider this one: What is your ultimate goal for your kids—immediate short–term comfort or long–term health and success? The A&E network broadcasts a show called "Intervention." Each episode presents a case of a family facing the crisis of having an adult member who's suffering with some form of addiction. In certain episodes, it's easy to pinpoint the root trauma that caused the addiction; the original source of dysfunctional behavior is the death of a parent, abuse as a child, or some other specific experience. In some cases, however, the family history seems to be rock–solid, with no apparent childhood trauma of any significance.

On the other hand, family members may be engaging in enabling practices that actually feed the self–destructive behaviors of the person with the addiction. Therefore, in every case the professional interventionist begins by working with the family as a whole to address any enabling practices on their part. Only then can the person with the addiction be brought into the process.

What determines the difference between helping our children and enabling them? *Helping* a child means facilitating something the child can't accomplish without assistance. For instance, if a child in college doesn't have the money to buy books, a parent might provide support in the form of financial help to make the purchase. *Enabling* means facilitating something the adult child can or should be doing inde-

> *Enabling is helping a person in a way that feeds the dysfunction. Helping is being there for someone in a way that does not support the dysfunction.*
>
> —*anonymous*

pendently. Suppose a child has dropped out of school because of negative behavior and won't even consider going back or trying to find a job, and the parents provide full financial support. Those parents are enabling their child's aimless lifestyle.

Enabling often starts out as helping. Allison Bottke, in her book, *Setting Boundaries with Your Adult Children,* writes,

> Somewhere along the parenting line, you [we!] set up a pattern of enabling that perhaps continues to this day. Your enabling may have been subconscious; you no doubt meant well (in fact, most enabling parents *do* mean well). But either way, the result is the same: you experience the pain of having an adult child who's out of control.

In essence, what we as parents can find ourselves doing is creating an environment in which our adult children can live comfortably while continuing in their negative behavior.

A parent who in some way enables an adult child to continue in destructive behaviors is creating short–term emotional relief and comfort at the price of long–term damage. In fact, parents may enjoy participating in such dysfunctional symbiotic relationships because this fulfills some emotional need of their own. When our children are crying out to us for resources or support, we experience a natural, instinctive impulse to provide whatever they say they need. Therefore, the shutting down of enabling practices with regard to an adult child's dysfunctional behaviors is typically a heart–wrenching exercise.

Dr. Bottke provides a list of questions for parents to use as they go through a process of self–evaluation to determine to what extent they may have become their adult child's enabler. The following hypothetical cases offer examples of what this kind of enabling looks like.

- Sarah no longer does anything to keep the house neat and clean, but you don't talk to her about it, because you don't want to start an argument. If she starts a project, you have to finish it. She had a pretty good job, but she hated it; a few times, you called in sick for her, even though she wasn't sick. She finally lost the job because she had missed so many days. You paid for her to take a training program at the local community college that would get her into a new line of work, but she dropped out after a couple weeks because it was so boring. Now Sarah has heard about a different program at a different school that sounds much more exciting, and she wants you to pay for that. You don't want to do it, because you don't trust her to stick with it, but you don't want to fight with her either.

- Ben has his own apartment. He has a job, but he's always coming to you to borrow money. He manages to pay his rent, but he is constantly afraid that the electricity or gas in his apartment will be turned off. Still, he buys every new video game that comes out and he bought a pair of sneakers that cost $500. He has never paid back a penny of what he owes you, and you really can't afford to keep giving him money. But you hate to make an issue of it, because you don't want to spoil your relationship with him. Lately, the problem with Ben has been getting worse. He's asking for more and more money, and if you hesitate to give it to him, he becomes angry. You're beginning to wonder if he might be using drugs. But if you say anything, he'll just get more angry. You feel like you're at your wits' end.

Close the Door of Enabling

Suppose that at some point you recognized that you were an enabler or in danger of becoming one. What do you do about it? The first step is a determined resolution to stop enabling dysfunctional behavior so that your child isn't still struggling, still living out the same negative patterns, two, five, ten years from now. That may sound easy, but it's often quite complex. You might need to seek out professional counseling for support and specific direction at this very early stage. If you're not sure whether or not you need this type of assistance, I suggest that you at least have an initial conversation with a professional who can help you make the determination.

After firmly setting your resolve to stop enabling, you begin initiating changes in your own patterns of behavior. You start by taking responsibility for your part in the decisions you and your child have made that have brought you to this point. In other words, you stop making excuses for yourself, just as you stop excusing your child's bad behavior. Keep in mind that you're working for the long-term health and security of your child, not today's emotional comfort. That's not to say that there may not be some legitimate historic reasons for the negative behavior; but now you must determine that you will no longer allow those past issues to dictate tomorrow's success or failure.

> *After living with their dysfunctional behavior for so many years ... people become invested in defending their dysfunctions rather than changing them.*
>
> —*Marshall Goldsmith*

Once the excuses are behind you, set behavioral boundaries and stick with them. This is one of the most difficult steps to accomplish at first because you are likely to think of a hundred reasons why you should give in "just this one time." Why do we discipline our young children? Because we love them and want them to be healthy, happy human beings and live a successful life. It's just the same with boundaries for our adult children; we want them to be healthier and happier human beings and to function successfully in society. The best way to establish a boundary is to learn the word NO. When your toddler reaches for a hot pot on the stove, you say "No." When your adult child is reaching out toward a dysfunctional lifestyle and seeks your help in maintaining it, your response is the same: "NO!!"

Forgive Them

"When children are little, they stomp on our feet. When they grow up, they stomp on our hearts." There's a lot of truth to this old saying. As a glass–half–full person, I like to believe that both kinds of stomping are done in innocence.

By far the most important thing we can do to help our adult children is to love them and forgive them. Yes, they are adults, but they are also still our children. It's our responsibility to do everything we can to help them to be successful for today and into the future. That responsibility includes refusing to accept irresponsibility in turn— refusing to enable our children's negative behaviors. But it also includes keeping the door open for loving and embracing them, just like the father of the Prodigal Son.

In this parable, the father grants his son an enormous sum of money, enough so that the young man can maintain a self–destructive lifestyle for a long period of time. When that lifestyle disintegrates and the son returns, ready to serve as a slave, his father meets him at the door and lavishes him with love and forgiveness. We need to be always ready to forgive our children their transgressions, never reminding them of their past dysfunctional behaviors—once those behaviors are truly in the past. What they need is our unreserved, deep parental love.

Out of Our House But Not Out of Our Hearts

Dear Lord,

*Our power is limited and our influence wanes
as our children grow into adults.*

*We commit them into Your gracious hands
and plead that You remember them.*

anonymous

11

The Hazards of Ministry

I bless the Lord who gives me counsel;
in the night also my heart instructs me.

I have set the Lord always before me;
because he is at my right hand,
I shall not be shaken.

Therefore my heart is glad,
and my whole being rejoices.

Psalm 16:7–9a (ESV)

The perfect pastor, as far as anyone knows, has yet to be born. If you spend any amount of time serving in a particular church, before long your people will know that God has sent to be their pastor one of those 'earthen vessels' the apostle Paul talks about. There is nothing like being a pastor of a local church to stretch even your most considerable gifts, and similarly, nothing quite like it to expose your frailties and weaknesses.

If you're like me, you found yourself nodding your head as you read this brief passage from *Help! I'm a Pastor*. Even the most talented Salvation Army officer suffers from the nagging reality of human imperfection. Any point of internal weakness can hamper the effectiveness of our ministry and even, in an extreme case, destroy our calling altogether. Officership is a tough business, fraught with many dangers. It's incumbent on each of us to recognize these dangers, including those that stem from our own weaknesses, and to develop strategies to help us avoid any possible pitfalls.

Inherent in our calling from God is a responsibility to grow in our discipleship to Christ, to be the best spiritual shepherds we can be for those within our appointment, and to care for our families. Our children are depending on us to live spiritually and morally healthy lives. If we're mired in sin or dysfunctional behaviors, how can we possibly help our children successfully navigate the storms that come their way due to the nature of our occupation? As we begin an examination of some of the hazards confronting us as ministers of the Gospel, keep this warning in mind: *"Be sober–minded; be watchful. Your adversary the devil prowls around like a roaring lion, seeking someone to devour."* 1 Peter 5:8 (ESV) That someone, Satan's potential prey, could be one of us or our children.

The Pastor's Journey

As my wife, Stacie—who was pregnant at the time—and I stepped out from behind the stage curtain at the Atlanta Civic Center on Commissioning day and walked toward the spotlight, making a beeline towards the commissioner, we were also taking the first steps of a life-long journey as officers. Every officer's passage through their various appointments is marked by different experiences. Some are unique to one particular officer; however, there are some common stressors and struggles that are an inherent to taking up the mantle of ministry.

One thought we cadets held in common throughout the entire meeting that day was the belief that we were going to make a dramatic impact in the world for the cause of Christ. None of us met the commissioner mid–stage with the idea that our ministry, our officership, or our family might crash and burn. We were certainly all convinced that we had at least developed a solid plan for our first week.

Day 1:   Unpack.

Day 2:   Meet everyone in town.

Day 3:   Meet everyone in the corps.

Day 4:   Solve all of the soldiers' problems.

Day 5:   Solve all the problems of the appointment.

Day 6:   Prepare an awe–inspiring sermon.

Day 7:   Preach the sermon in such a way that it would be talked about for generations.

This is obviously hyperbole, but it illustrates some of the confidence and vigor we felt on our Commissioning day. Stacie and I were sure of achieving nothing less than spiritual excellence. After all, I was the child of missionary officer parents, so I knew exactly what to expect as an officer. That also meant that I'd never make the same mistakes my parents had made—from my perspective, at least—as I was growing up. Because I had my life as an officer all figured out, I could focus all my energies on fixing the world. I believed this to be true all the way up to the point when I crashed into my first appointment. After many years of hard–learned lessons, I now understand that there's only way to come to understand and appreciate the pressures and hazards that confront corps officers and their families: by experience.

A foundational study on this subject was conducted by Fuller Theological Seminary in the late 1980s. Among the findings:

- By far the great majority of pastors reported working a longer–than–normal workweek.

- Most pastors said they believed their ministry had had a negative effect on their families, and a substantial portion said that being in ministry was a hazard to their families.

- Roughly half of the pastors reported feeling unable to meet the needs of the job.

- More than two–thirds testified to having a lower self–image since being in pastoral ministry than when they started.

- More than two–thirds did not have someone they considered a close friend.

  » Two–thirds said that church members expected ministers and their families to live at a higher moral standard than them.

  » Nearly half reported a serious conflict with a parishioner at least once a month.

- More than one–third admitted being involved in inappropriate sexual behavior with someone in their congregation.

Admittedly, this information is now somewhat out of date, and the percentages may have changed; but there's little doubt that the general picture remains the same. In their book, *Pastors at Greater Risk*—published in 2003—London and Wiseman list the "8 top areas of stress for pastors (in random order): time, boundaries, isolation, conflict, mobility, life in parsonage, concern for children and spouse, and family dynamics."

It seems that this life to which God has called us to is more than just a little dangerous. Don't lose heart, however; we are far from a lost cause. *"The one who is in you is greater than the one who is in the world."* 1 John 4:4 (CEB) On the other hand, this truth from God's Word in no way reduces our responsibility to be wise and vigilant with respect to the dangers we face. Our ministry and our families are precious gifts from God, and we have a responsibility to guard them and help them to grow in the light of God. Let's explore some of the hazards we face.

Time

The Barna Group, which conducts ongoing research on various aspects of the state of evangelical church life in America, reported: "Our studies show that church-goers expect their pastor to juggle an average of 16 major tasks. That's a recipe for failure—nobody can

> *The high demands of time and energy required in my appointment continue to escalate, and it has taken a toll on health and well-being. I blame me for not being disciplined enough to take better care of myself. Now I'm practically 'fried.'*
>
> —an officer

handle the wide range of responsibilities that people expect pastors to master."

Clearly one of the chief obstacles pastors encounter and one of the major issues we as officers are confronted with is that there is simply never enough time. This is especially true during the months of November and December, when our lives are swallowed up by a deluge of seasonal responsibilities, but it is a year-round problem. As we are being squeezed from every direction, the temptation is to steal time from our families in order to measure up to all the other officers. The fact is that every officer is confronted with myriad time demands, so you're not alone. And remember: your family is your initial pastoral responsibility and should never be neglected or placed on a sacrificial altar.

Consider these thoughts from London and Wiseman, in their book, *Your Pastor Is an Endangered Species:*

> Pastors live in a world that never stops, where the light never goes out, and where the average work week is between fifty–five and seventy–five hours. Pastors dwell in a world of the unfinished tyranny, where they can't shut the door, walk out of the office, or know something is completely finished. There's always another Bible study, sermon, phone call, committee, hospital call, home visit, [McWilliams: kettle run, client issue, employee problem, fundraiser, board meeting, organizational report], or gathering clamoring for attention. When someone dies or gets married or is hospitalized, the well–crafted schedule has to be abandoned and caught up later. Sometime later is a long time in coming. Pastors live in a world of guilt about their families. Pastors live in a world of decreasing approval. They serve in a 'me–centered' world where church members and others are becoming more apathetic.

As officers, we can offer up a chorus of *amens* to these words. This is how we live. Now, as an exercise, reread the quote; as you read, consider how your child might view your allotments of personal time and energy.

If you're unable to discern how to juggle your organizational, ministry, and familial responsibilities properly, please reach out to the Lord for wisdom. His promise to provide it is set forth in James 1:5, nicely expressed in the Common English Bible (CEB) version: *"Anyone who needs wisdom should ask God, whose very nature is to give to everyone without a second thought, without keeping score. Wisdom will certainly be given to those who ask."* Also, look to officers who are successful time managers; ask them for their wise counsel.

Unreasonable Expectations

Pastors, particularly those within Army ranks, are expected to be as equally skilled at business administration, finance, and human resources as they

> *So many times I feel that I am not qualified for this calling. I am also having a hard time finding a balance for it all.*
>
> —*an officer*

are at preaching, counseling, and shepherding a flock. Craig Ellison and William Mattila describe feelings of

163

inadequacy as one of the "Top five most identifiable issues of ministry leadership burnout."

I'll never forget sitting at my desk in my first appointment and asking my wife if we had attended the right training college, not because being at the school wasn't a great experience, but because there's no way that every contingency can be taught in two years. There are so many different areas in which we as officers are expected to be experts and so many different issues we are required to handle on a daily basis that to be proficient in everything would be an amazing feat. Probably all of us have felt at some point like we've been pushed into the deep end of the pool to learn how to swim. During my first days of command, I couldn't even decide which mail I was supposed to keep, which to file, and which to trash. So for the first year of my officership, I filed everything, even the sale flyers!

A report on a national study of ministers from six different denominations described pastors as "Being in the 'holy crossfire,' as the clergyperson and his family attempt to juggle the expectations of self, congregation, denomination, and God." There are many days in the life of a corps officer—while we're busy receiving phone calls from donors, dealing with employee issues, conducting corps meetings, working to get reports in on time, and writing emails concerning financial or program problems—when it would be easy for us to skip our familial responsibilities. The pressures exerted by the expectations associated with our work can be stifling and ultimately destructive if we're not careful to address them properly.

In most literature focused on the hazards of ministry, authors describe the harm that can be caused by excessive expectations placed not only on pas-

> *As a new officer, it is often difficult to find a balance between being a pastor and administrator.*
>
> *—an officer*

tors, but also on their families. The idea of familial perfection because of congregational expectations can be especially destructive to our children. Bruce Hardy, in a journal article entitled "Pastoral Care with Clergy Children," wrote: "Clergy children feel pressured to behave like polished saints or seasoned disciples."

Dysfunctional People

Another source of officer pressure is working closely with dysfunctional people. Dysfunction in this case doesn't necessarily mean severe mental problems; it can refer to people who are suffering emotionally due to difficult experiences. There are those who are attracted to a spiritual life through our social services because of enduring personal issues, hurts, or deficiencies within themselves. As a church, we provide hope, socialization, community, and purpose to many people who are desperately in need of these influences. Unfortunately, sometimes these same people create extreme conflict and disruption within the church body—as well as a significant emotional drain on the officer.

In *Clergy Killers*, Lloyd Rediger wrote, "The abuse of clergy is often led by a person with antisocial or borderline personality disorders who has consciously or unconsciously aligned herself or himself with evil. Disordered people are particularly capable of manipulating naïve or other disordered persons into following their pathological agenda." Churches that intentionally minister to the least and lost, as The Salvation Army does, are the most susceptible to these dysfunctional influences.

Officership is not easy. The demands can be unreal and taxing at times. It takes a toll on one's physical, emotional and spiritual life, not to mention marriages and parent/child relationships.

—an officer

Jesus said, *"I am sending you out as sheep in the midst of wolves, so be wise as serpents and innocent as doves."* Matthew 10:16 (ESV)

There can also be some soldiers who create high levels of stress and cause emotional drain on the officer. Marshall Shelley called these people *Well–Intentioned Dragons*.

> Within the church, they are often sincere, well–meaning saints, but they leave ulcers, strained relationships, and hard feelings in their wake. They don't consider themselves difficult people.... They are not naturally rebellious or pathological; they are loyal church members, convinced they're serving God, but they wind up doing more harm than good.

We should never shy away from ministering to the least, lost, or dysfunctional, but we should be aware of what the cost can be to ourselves and our families.

Isolation

The role of pastor in any denomination carries with it some level of isolation. People who have chosen this path never enjoy the luxury of being able to let their guard down. This inevitably creates walls that hinder relationships with the people around them, leading to feelings of distinct isolation. Officers who serve in The Salvation Army are continually subject to an expectation of relocation at some unknown future date; this increases their isolation to an even higher level, because they are conditioned to create relationships with equally unknown expiration dates. Once officers have formed deep, meaningful relationships in one appointment only to have those roots torn up, they are far less ready to sink roots as deeply again. Whether the officers are consciously aware of this or not, when friendships are broken and the same thing is almost certain to happen again, a reactive emotional defense mechanism is engaged.

> *The fears of moving, repercussions, bad reputation or lack of help forces officers to not share concerns, problems and stumbling blocks.*
>
> —*an officer*

Confronted with this conditioning, officers respond in different ways, based on past experiences and innate personality. Many officers throw themselves into an exclusive Salvation Army–specific sphere in which they engage in deep friendships only with other officers. Others live out their lives with nothing more than shallow friendships. Still others withdraw and struggle with ever–present feelings of isolation and loneliness.

This emotional separation can detach ministers not only from their congregants, but also from their colleagues and peers. A study of Methodist ministers revealed the following:

Skilled at meeting the needs of others, clergy seem to be far less able to take care of themselves. In the midst of a crowd of parishioners, clergy often find themselves to be lonely. The ministers studied seem to have difficulty in sharing their deepest needs, joys, concerns and sorrows with others, including clergy peers. Those who can listen to their parishioners unburdening their souls are often unable to do so themselves. Respondents reported a great reluctance to share deeply and openly with peers (despite frequent associations through meetings and nominal support groups), citing a lack of trust and feelings of competition. "What if I reveal my true self to a colleague, and then he or she becomes my next district superintendent?" was a question asked a number of times. Confidentiality is also a crucial issue; there was some feeling that news travels fast and far on the clerical grapevine.

Intimacy and emotional isolation seem to be problems that go beyond the issue of trust. Many clergy are fearful of becoming 'too involved' in friendships with either laity or other clergy, one reason being the possibility of having to move away from these relationships. Both clergy and spouses said they have experienced too many losses to want to invest themselves in new friendships and run the risk of more pain.

As bad as it is for us as officers to feel this sense of isolation, it's much worse for our children. As has been made abundantly clear in this book, friendships and the opinions of peers are extremely important to kids. It can be terrifying for them to be out in the "social cold."

Organizational Ambition and Prestige

Positional ambition is a potential hazard that is inherent to serving within a hierarchical organization. For some officers, positions of power can become an all–consuming ambition, so that they focus their strength and efforts on climbing the organizational ladder. One consequence is that our families can find themselves being left behind as we pursue personal glory. We busy ourselves with seeking out appointments that we believe will enhance our standing without considering whether or not this next move will be detrimental to our children.

An ambition–driven focus is often associated with a view of position as a measure of personal success in ministry. If not being appointed to a high–prestige position makes an officer feel like a failure, this is likely to create an attitude of resentment toward the organization—which will almost certainly affect the officer's ministry and family. Salvation Army officers are not

> *I don't want others to know that I'm a failure.*
>
> *—an officer*

alone in struggling with this issue. The study of Methodist ministers mentioned earlier found, "There is considerable anxiety about how one will fare in the United Methodist appointive system. There is often a tendency, accompanied by a great deal of anger, to blame one's ills on the system."

Ambition can create a false sense within ourselves of who we are and what attributes we bring to the ministry table. Robert Burns, the great Scottish poet, wrote the plea (as it would be in modern English), "Oh would some Power the gift give us, to see ourselves as others see us!" Every officer is unique and specially gifted. The fact that the Lord has touched our lives and called us to this ministry should be enough to create a spirit of awe and gratitude within each of us. However, if we've convinced ourselves, because of our organizational ambition, that we "deserve" appointment A, and then find ourselves being moved to appointment B, Satan can use this personal disappointment to embitter our spirit toward that new command. The terrible result of such disillusionment can be that everyone within that ministry context, including our families, will receive from us only a shell of what we could have presented to them as their pastors.

As officers and shepherds in Salvation Army ministry, we need to understand that our vocation brings with it many inherent difficulties. We face spiritual attack as well as organizational, congregational, community, and familial expectations that can create high levels of stress potentially leading to burnout. For the sake of our children, who are our lifestyle partners and whom we deeply desire to see come to a knowledge of the loving grace of our Lord Jesus Christ in their own lives, we need to vigilantly keep our personal and familial foundations rock–solid. This means maintaining a vibrant spiritual walk and maintaining a fully balanced life. If we follow this pattern, we give our children as well as ourselves the best chance to be happy, fulfilled, and successful.

Before Thy face, dear Lord,
Myself I want to see;
And while I every question sing,
I want to answer Thee.

The Hazards of Ministry

While I speak to Thee,
Lord, Thy goodness show;
Am I what I ought to be?

O Savior, let me know.

Am I what once I was?

Have I that ground maintained
Wherein I walked in power with Thee,
And Thou my soul sustained?

Have I a truthful heart,
A conscience keen to feel
The baseness of a false excuse,
The touch of aught unreal?

Have I the zeal I had
When Thou didst me ordain
To preach Thy Word and seek the lost,
Or do I feel it pain?

O Lord, if I am wrong,
I will not grieve Thee more
By doubting Thy great love and power
To make and keep me pure.

Herbert Booth

(The Song Book of The Salvation Army #697)

12

Living in Balance

The Lord is my rock and my fortress and my deliverer,
my God, my rock, in whom I take refuge,
my shield, and the horn of my salvation,
my stronghold and my refuge, my savior;
you save me from violence.

I call upon the Lord, who is worthy to be praised,
and I am saved from my enemies.

2 Samuel 22:2–4 (ESV)

A shepherd who kept his sheep near the sea one day drove them down to the shore. The sea lay before him, all calm and smooth, and of an enchanting blue. He longed to sail away, to see other lands, to become rich through commerce. So he sold all his flock, bought a small ship, loaded her with a cargo of dates, and set sail. But a very great tempest quickly came on, and with the ship in danger of sinking, he threw all his mer-chandise overboard, and barely escaped with his life. Once back on land, he took work watching over the sheep he once had owned and in the course of time, by care and frugality, again became possessed of some wealth. He found himself one day on that selfsame shore, looking out upon the calm blue sea. But he cried out, 'Deceitful and tempting element! Do not try to engage me a second time. Others may confide their treasure to your treacherous care, but never will I trust your faithless charm again.'

Like all of Aesop's fables, this one makes a point. The shepherd was sure he had found the way to a life of pleasure and riches. He didn't count on the problems he might face.

Having children and raising a family may look won-derful—even easy—from the outside, but parents know that it entails facing storms of many different kinds. This doesn't mean that we regret embarking on the voyage of parenthood; the joy our children bring us far outweighs the stresses and strains. It does mean that we need to be prepared to navigate these times of tumultuous wind and waves, especially those that involve our children— and, for us as Salvation Army officers, most particularly those that are brought on by our ministry lifestyle of frequent changes of appointment.

When a ship encounters a storm, its best defense against being capsized is its overall balance. For this reason, ships are equipped with pumps that can expel water from the hull or take in water, depending on what is needed to maintain balance. If a ship is out of balance when it encounters a storm, it can capsize, and tragedy may ensue. The same principle applies to us. When we're transferred, it creates a storm that can buffet the family ship. The best defense we have against capsizing is a firmly established balance in our lives.

The life of each one of us as Salvation Army officers is made up of four primary aspects: God, self, family, and ministry. All of these need to be in harmony. When we fail to invest ourselves in any one of them, that part will suffer, negatively affecting all the other parts. For a healthy, balanced life, we need to pour our time and energies into all of them.

A Life in Balance

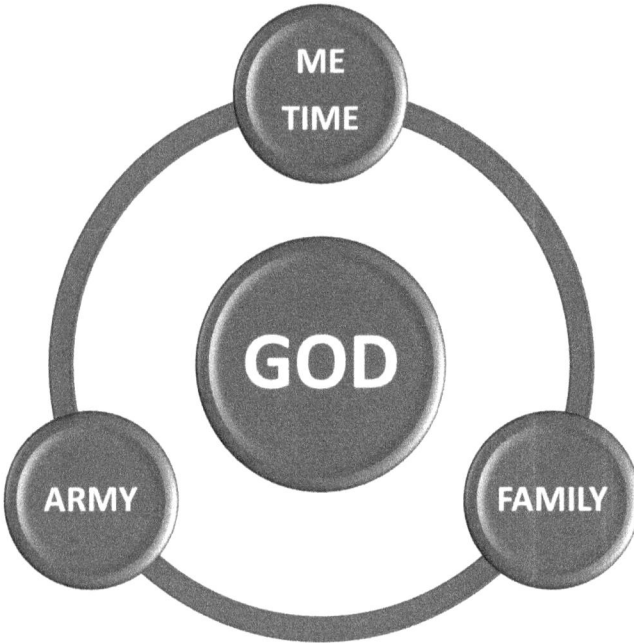

It seems only right that we as pastors would be espousing the need for a balanced life. After all, balance is biblical. When God created the world in which we live, He placed everything in perfect balance so that His creation could flourish. All was well until Adam and Eve decided that they would be better off listening to Satan and their own selfish desires than to God. Ever since that fateful moment, people have had to fight to re–establish a sense of personal and spiritual balance. Everything around us functions better when it's in balance, and yet the world we live in seems to be constantly drawing us toward imbalance.

A Balanced Spiritual Life

The centerpiece of a balanced life is God, and only God. He should be the focus of our worship and the source of our stability and power. If God is not at the center of our personal lives, Army ministry, and familial relationships, we have no chance of achieving a balanced life marked by peace and contentment. All three of the other important aspects of our existence depend on, feed from, and are nourished by Him. To neglect our spiritual connection with God is to rob every other part and person in our lives.

If you haven't stopped to ponder this in quite a while, do it now: God, the Creator, Preserver, and Governor of all things, wants more than anything to be in a personal relationship with each one of us! Like any relationship, this one requires an investment from both parties. And we have a choice of how much we are willing to invest. We can fake a bond with God and still be officers. We can pronounce our personal holiness to whoever will listen, yet never give ourselves fully over to His grace. We can make the initial commitment and then starve the relationship by neglecting to invest our time and energies into it. Or we can live our lives in the way that we proclaim that others should, and present to God our sincere love, time, and effort. Whichever way we choose to live out our officership, both God and our family will know. *"Everyone's path is straight in their own eyes, but the Lord weighs the heart."* Proverbs 21:2 (CEB)

I would like to believe that being ministers of the Gospel and knowing about our ultimate future would be enough to drive us to our knees. *"I'm coming soon. My reward is with me, to repay all people as their actions deserve."* Revelation 22:12 (CEB) Do Jesus' words sound more like a warning or more like a glorious, joy-inspiring promise?

We as parents have a particular motivation to seek an ever-deepening spiritual relationship with God, one of vital importance. We provide the starting point of our children's spiritual training and their attitudes with respect to biblical faith and ministry. If we model a life that is spiritually shallow or false, they will begin from there. Conversely, dynamic spiritual parents will convey the importance of godliness to them.

In addition, the closer our walk with the Lord, the clearer and more powerful our prayers for our children will be. *"We receive from him whatever we ask, be-*

cause we obey his commandments and do what pleases him…. All who obey his commandments abide in him, and he abides in them. And by this we know that he abides in us, by the Spirit that he has given us." 1 John 3:22, 24 (NRSV) I believe that if we as parents are not seeking an ever–deepening relationship with God, we are betraying our children, because our prayers for them are muted in power and authority. I believe that a vibrant spiritual life breeds power in prayer with which to undergird our children. A dead spiritual life in which the commands of God are ignored offers no such power.

A Balanced Me

"Eat your broccoli. It's good for you. You can't live on just ice cream!" I heard this as a young boy, and I couldn't have disagreed more. After all, ice cream is a food, so why couldn't we live on a diet made up of different flavors of ice cream? My mother knew better— that to grow up and become a healthy adult, I needed a balanced diet made up of various types of nutrients. Unfortunately for me, she was a walking nutrition pyramid chart. I've since learned that this principle of successful living through balance doesn't apply only to our food choices. Living out of balance in any one area—physical, emotional, or spiritual—can lead to personal stress and dysfunction and affect our families as well.

> *I need help. Keeping a healthy balance between work, family life, and personal life is a constant challenge. Guilt plays havoc on me when I can't fulfill my motherly roles as well as my officer roles.*
>
> *—an officer*

William Booth said, "We are not sent to minister to a congregation and be content if we keep things going. We are sent to make war … and to stop short of nothing but the subjugation of the world to the sway of the Lord Jesus." As Salvation Army officers, we shouldn't expect to fight in such a dramatic conflict and walk away without any scars. As parents, however, it's our sincere desire that these wounds won't be visited upon our children. To even begin to fulfill this desire, we must address the issue of stability and balance in our own personal lives.

Richard and Linda Eyre write,

> The remarkable thing about doing the right things for yourself is that it is the most unselfish thing you can do. We all know that is true—when we stop to think about it. We can do so much more for others when we take care of ourselves. It is when our health is good, when we feel secure, when we are

rested, when we are stimulated that we find the inclination and the insight necessary to help others.

Therefore, as tempting as it might be to define a successful ministry as one that keeps us living on the edge of burnout, don't do it. STOP! Burning ourselves out in the name of God will not be rewarded with a badge of spiritual honor. I can't help but wonder how many officers have been lost through the years because they didn't take care of their own emotional and spiritual needs.

If you should find yourself living that way, feeling like you are constantly on the edge of burnout, or if it appears that your children may be suffering from your lack of emotional balance, how do you bring yourself into equilibrium? A good first step is to sit down with your family for an honest inventory of your life, taking into account such matters as the unavoidable demands on your time and the needs of the family. For best results, this assessment should include taking a calendar and physically sketching out how you spend your time. Doing this with the whole family present establishes a kind of accountability with respect to evaluating your time expenditures.

Once you have determined that you're living out of balance and determined where you have been over-spending—or underspending—your time, you can set begin to make adjustments in your schedule, ensuring effective allotment of time each week for spiritual formation, yourself, family interaction, and active ministry. This is explored in further detail at the end of this chapter.

Rest and Restoration

Underpinning the entire structure of personal balance is rest. We can create and implement brilliant schemes for balancing our lives, but in the absence of proper rest, they are destined to fail. There are a couple of different aspects to resting that are important for us to monitor and adhere to. The first is actual sleep. It is a cruel irony that when the pressures of life and ministry are at their height, we have the most trouble being able to sleep properly. When we operate without adequate sleep, the problems seem to grow, which robs us of more restful sleep, which increases our level of anxiety, which robs us of more restful sleep—and so on. What a vicious cycle!

The Cleveland Clinic Brain and Spine Team released a short list of what happens to us when we don't get enough sleep:

- Lack of alertness
- Impaired memory
- Relationship stress

- Poorer quality of daily life
- Greater likelihood of car accidents

I would add a related item: impaired judgement. Consider this list being applied to you or your children when the environmental stress around you increases due to a move. Please, do what you can to get enough sleep, even in the midst of tumultuous times.

Rest doesn't apply only to physical sleep. It's also important that we rest from the strains and rigors of our day–to–day ministries. *"Jesus Himself would often slip away to the wilderness and pray."* Luke 5:16 (NASB) When Jesus got away from His physical ministry to the crowds, He spent time re–energizing and refocusing His spiritual and familial connections without distraction. When we read this Scripture, we might think only about Jesus' spiritual connection with the Father, which was of course vitally important. However, He was also communing with *His* Father, interacting with the Person closest to Him. When we get away from the rigors of our appointments, we need to take advantage of this time to connect and de-

> *I'm very tired. I love more than anything what I do. I'm just tired. I know that my exhaustion contributes to a 'less than well–done' job.*
>
> *—an officer*

velop our relationship with God and with our families. The effort will help us to create and maintain a strong, balanced familial and spiritual foundation.

I know well the feelings we as officers can carry: "My appointment will fall apart without me." But what good are you to your appointment and to your family if you're the one who falls apart? Leave your computer and cellphone behind and go to the wilderness by yourself to commune with God, or with your family for a true bonding experience. Your appointment will survive.

A Balanced Family

As we drive around the country, it's common to see animal crossing signs on the side of the highway. They're usually yellow, with the form of an animal in black—a jumping deer, for example, warning us to be cautious and on the lookout for deer crossing the road. There are other animal crossing signs as well, for cattle, horses, bears, and in Florida, alligators. However, I've never seen an animal standing at one of these signs waiting to cross the road. It would be nice if the animals would use these signs

> *It is difficult most of the time to balance being a wife, mother, and officer, which plays into the family dynamics.*
>
> *—an officer*

as road crossing points, but they just chaotically spring out in front of a driver anywhere the mood strikes them. The same could be said about family life. It would be extremely convenient if our children would confine their problems and crises to certain designated days and times. Unfortunately, that's not the way it is.

This chaotic disorder means that we need to constantly be prepared for whatever our children may face by monitoring their behaviors. Our state of preparation is especially critical in determining how our children will cope when confronted with the emotional turbulence of a move. How well we've succeeded in establishing a familial foundation that is emotionally and spiritually firm will be fully exposed when confronted with this transition.

Hans V. Ritschard has offered a number of criteria for distinguishing between healthy and unhealthy family lifestyles. For example:

- Attitudes. Do family members enjoy being together? Do they express affection toward one another? Do they have a clear sense of "family"?

- Actions. Do family members communicate openly with one another? Do any family members manifest aggression toward others, physically or verbally?

- Issues. Are problems acknowledged or swept under the rug? Are the means of addressing them oriented toward solutions or toward blame?

I would add some other criteria, especially for officers' families:

- Attitudes. Is the family atmosphere actively spiritual? Are the lives of family members centered on God or on themselves? Are moral standards strictly upheld, or not taken too seriously?

- Actions. Do family members readily forgive each other when wronged? Are children genuine participants in family decision making?

- Emotional health. Do some members display dysfunctional behaviors or signs of emotional instability? How are these problems addressed?

For a moment, consider your family's interactions in light of these criteria. As a parent, do you feel that you are creating a balanced, healthy environment in which your children can grow and learn? Your children look to you as a model for their own lives. Are you setting them up for success or failure? As officers and parents, we need to be honest about our own emotional and spiritual deficiencies and work to correct those areas. Only then can we expect our children to respond favorably to our loving correction and guidance.

A Balanced Ministry

Our ministry is far more than fundraising, social services, and corps programming.

> *For we do not wrestle against flesh and blood, but against the rulers, against the authorities, against the cosmic powers over this present darkness, against the spiritual forces of evil in the heavenly places. Therefore take up the whole armor of God, that you may be able to withstand in the evil day, and having done all, to stand firm."*
> Ephesians 6:12–13 (ESV)

A successful ministry is based on spiritual excellence and endurance. In order for us to participate in a spiritual battle, we have to be spiritually in tune with God. If we wear organizational eyeglasses—viewing our overall spirituality and the successful fulfillment of our godly calling from an organizational perspective—we will tend to think that we're pleasing God when our stats are up and our finances are flying high. These are certainly worthy goals, but are they the measure of

God's pleasure? Couldn't a secular MBA (or a secular circus performer!) also increase stats and finances?

A better pair of eyeglasses to wear would focus on fulfilling the pleasure of God with our hearts and not just our hands. These "servant glasses" would see spiritual success as the embracing and implementing of God's commandments. "If you keep my commandments, you will abide in my love, just as I have kept my Father's commandments and abide in his love." John 15:10 (ESV) We can increase stats and not love people, or we can be a financial whiz and not love God. Pleasing God is a heart matter, not one of personal accomplishment. God forbid that these words should ever apply to us: "These people honor me with their lips, but their hearts are far from me." Matthew 15:8 (NIV)

> As Christians we are called to do all things to the glory of God, including—perhaps especially—our work.
>
> —Ravi Zacharias

There's an age–old philosophical question that has been applied in all sorts of situations: "Which came first, the chicken or the egg?" Here's an answer to a more important question, an answer that should be on the lips of every Salvation Army officer: "My spiritual faith and my righteous walk come first, and out of that my ministry can flourish." It must never be, "My stats and finances flourish, so my spiritual walk can be whatever I want it to be." Always remember that our children are growing up in a dark, sinful world. They're in desperate need of parents who are sold out for, and rest upon, a solid spiritual foundation.

Out of Balance

If we're honest with ourselves, we know when we're not living in balance. We know if we're not spending enough quality time with God or with our family. If we're *really* honest, we know when we aren't getting enough sleep or when we haven't spent enough time relaxing. Just take a moment and think through the various areas of your life to determine which ones are withering and which are healthy. Have you ever seen a picture of yourself and been horrified at some glaring thing you hate about "you"? It's a terrible moment of realization. Unfortunately, we aren't generally able to see ourselves as others see us, or as we truly are. Sometimes it takes one of those "photographic moments" to jar us into the realization that something would have to change for us to be the person we think we are or want to be.

In relation to living in balance, a photographic moment can come from the words and actions of people around us. For example, if your children are complaining that you spend too much time at the office, and that

> *I struggle to get the 'required' things done in 50+ hours of officer time. Work on sermons and care for the congregation either takes away from family time or sleep time. All of this makes me ill–tempered with my wife and child.*
>
> —an officer

when you come home all you talk about is business, they're showing you a photograph of your family/ministry balance. If your spouse is complaining that you never spend quality time alone, that's a photograph telling you that you need to make a life adjustment.

Another kind of photographic moment, one that deserves to be taken very seriously, can present itself in the form of a problem arising in the life of someone who is dear to us. For example, if our children are exhibiting negative behaviors, that should jolt us into analyzing the amount of quality time we spend with them. A simple adjustment in how—and, especially, how much—we interact with our family can make a world of difference in their lives, and in ours.

Back in Balance

When I was in college, I had the idea that if I still had a check in my checkbook, I must still have money. I soon found myself in financial trouble because I was bouncing checks. There's nothing like paying an extra $25 bank fee and $10 store fee for an $8 shirt. What I didn't realize was that I needed to live by a budget in order to experience a successful financial life.

Our time allotment is just like our income. It's limited, and we have to be intentional in how we spend it. There are those four areas of our lives in which we must spend some of our quality time in order to live in balance: God, ourselves, family, and ministry. If we aren't intentional about budgeting our time, some area will probably end up being shortchanged.

Here's a practical idea: For one week, carry around a little journal and keep track of how you spend your quality time in relation to God, your family, yourself, and your appointment. No cheating now; don't change your routine or count one activity in several categories. Remember that we're talking about real quality time. You might as well be honest with this exercise as only you—and God, of course—will know the truth of your findings. At the end of the week, check your journal to see who might feel left out or cheated, if anyone. Where is the imbalance in your life?

Once you have discovered that you're living out of balance and determined where you have been over-spending—or underspending—your time, you can establish a schedule with time expenditure allotments for spiritual formation, yourself, family interaction, and active ministry. Then you need to ensure the success of your plan by establishing boundaries around it. A good way for us as parents to think about boundaries is to look at how they work with toddlers. As soon as our children become mobile, we go through the house working to baby–proof it. Then we establish boundaries around the secured area, often setting up barriers in order to ensure a safe zone. Once these lines of demarcation have been set for our toddler, we vigilantly watch to ensure that these barriers are maintained, always ready with the word NO!

What works for a toddler will work for you as well. You start by setting up a schedule that will allow you to experience balance with respect to the different important areas of your life. Next you establish boundaries around this plan and vigilantly monitor them. Then you have to be disciplined enough to say NO when you are tempted to habitually violate the plan. To fail to set proper boundaries, or to live outside the boundaries we set, invites imbalance, undue stress, and burnout. Try to remember that it was the Lord who called us to work in

His Kingdom vineyard. He didn't call us to failure and burnout, but to work for His glory until the end of our race.

Of course, this is a very simplified metaphor; our lives are in constant flux. However, the central principle is sound. As our lives, appointments, and families change, we need to constantly re–evaluate and re–establish our boundaries to meet the new demands. For example, we know which evenings are dedicated to corps programs; therefore, we know which evenings we can dedicate to spending fun time with our children and what time we have for ourselves to engage in personal spiritual development or to watch our favorite TV show. When we change appointments, the midweek service may shift from Tuesday night to Wednesday night. So we adjust our schedule, moving our parent–child banana split night from Wednesday to Tuesday.

Once we've made these adjustments, our work is not finished. Just as with our finances, our time budgets need to be constantly monitored, and amendments will

Setting boundaries is a way of caring for my family, my ministry, and myself. It doesn't make me mean, selfish, or uncaring, it means that I care enough about you to make sure that I'm presenting my best self before you.

—anonymous

have to be made as time expenditures arise unexpect-edly. And we shouldn't feel guilty about making these adjustments; we as well as our families deserve the gift of our time. What we should feel guilty about is not ex-pending our time in a way that maximizes our mental, physical, and spiritual health, the health and balance of our family, and our offering to God in ministry.

> *Precious Lord, take my hand,*
> *lead me on, let me stand,*
> *I am tired, I am weak, I am worn;*
> *Through the storm, through the night,*
> *lead me on to the light.*

> *Take my hand, precious Lord,*
> *lead me home.*

> *When my way grows drear,*
> *precious Lord, linger near,*
> *When my life is almost gone;*
> *Hear my cry, hear my call,*
> *hold my hand lest I fall.*

> *Take my hand, precious Lord,*
> *lead me home.*

> *When the darkness appears*
> *and the night draws near,*

And the day is past and gone;
At the river I stand,
guide my feet, hold my hand.

Take my hand, precious Lord,
lead me home.

Thomas A. Dorsey

13

A Conclusion to the Matter

*I have no greater joy than to hear
that my children are walking in the truth.*

3 John 4 (ESV)

From the moment our children are conceived, they are the most precious earthly gifts God has given us. They need our nurture and our love. As an officer of The Salvation Army, you are a precious gift given by God to the world to lift up the least and spread the Gospel to the lost. You also require nurture and love. Please take care of yourself and your family.

In our training session, among the people with whom my wife and I were commissioned as officers, we have so far experienced an attrition rate of over

50 percent. A majority of our class, people who professed a calling from God upon their lives to serve Him through the work of the Army, are no longer standing in the breach as officers. A few of these individuals left the work because of no fault of their own, but most are just gone, many with their marriages split. Were their callings temporary or misplaced, or did the pressures of life in ministry and the spiritual warfare we are engaged in take its toll? Only God and these people know the answer. However, if we lost any of them because they failed to take care of themselves or their families, we need to fight tooth and nail to try and ensure that that kind of loss doesn't happen again.

Ten Commandments for Parents in Ministry

I can't think of a better way to close this book than with some wisdom from the writings of Donald A. Lichi, a psychologist at EMERGE Counseling Services, a growing Christ-centered mental health facility:

> Research suggests that growing up in a ministry home has risks and rewards. The rewards include well-developed social skills, opportunities for interaction with spiritual leaders, and resiliency. On the other hand, it is well-documented that ministers' chil-

dren are under a microscope and are often held to higher standards than other children. Based on God's commands to Moses, here are some guidelines for the pastor in the role of parent:

1. You shall not make your ministry a higher priority than God and your family. Instead, you shall remember that your first call is to be a minister to your family as a spouse and a parent.

2. You shall not make idols for yourself. Remember to use things and love people, not the other way around. Model for your children a healthy perspective on material things as well as place a higher value on relationships.

3. You shall not misuse the name of the Lord your God. Instead, you shall model for your children a healthy submission to God's authority and submission to other constituted authorities. Children need to learn that all are under authority. This structure is God's provision for our guidance and safety.

4. You shall keep a day of the week as your day off. This Sabbath is a day to rest, refresh, renew, and recreate. Model for your children that the world (and ministry) goes on without you and that a Sabbath is a gift of God.

5. You shall honor your own parents. This models for your children a healthy intergenerational perspective of care and sacrificial living.

6. You shall not murder. In practical ways you shall model for your children how to bless those who curse you, do good to those who despitefully use you and speak well of those who speak ill of you. Furthermore, you shall model a forgiving spirit.

7. You shall not commit adultery. You shall model for your children that you are still madly in love with your spouse. This includes loving eye contact and gestures, affirming words, thoughtfulness, and couple time together away from the children.

8. You shall not steal. You shall model for your children a spirit of generosity, giving, and serving.

9. You shall not give false testimony against your neighbor. You shall model the value of building trusting relationships and nurturing several close friendships.

10. You shall not covet. You shall model a lifestyle that is devoid of complaint and one that exemplifies contentment with God's provision.

A Prayer for You

Please accept this prayer over you and your family. God bless you, your family, and your ministry.

Dearest Lord,

In the name of Jesus Christ, I approach Your throne.

Please send Your Holy Spirit to touch the life of every officer today.

Fill them with Your presence and solidify their hearts to Your glory.

Place a protection around them and their ministry while serving on the battlefield.

Don't Let Them Drown

May You be glorified!

Send Your Spirit to touch their families as well.

*Bless and protect their marriages and their children
from the evil one and from the world.*

*Give them the wisdom and guidance they need
to be the very best*

*fathers, mothers, husbands, wives, and children
You would have them be.*

*Provide comfort, help, rest, assurance,
and whatever else their souls require.*

May You be glorified!

Amen

For Further Reading

Jane Adams, *When Our Grown Kids Disappoint Us: Letting Go of Their Problems, Loving Them Anyway.* Free Press, 2008.

Richard Armstrong and Kirk Morledge, *Help! I'm a Pastor: A Guide to Parish Ministry.* Westminster John Knox Press, 2005.

Allison Bottke, *Setting Boundaries with Your Adult Children: Six Steps to Hope and Healing for Struggling Parents.* Harvest House Publishers, 2008.

William Bridges and Susan Bridges, *Managing Transitions: Making the Most of Change.* Da Capo Lifelong Books, 2017.

Lori C. Burgan, *Moving with Kids: 25 Ways to Ease Your Family's Transition to a New Home.* Harvard Common Press, 2007.

R. Hoge Dean and Jacqueline E. Wenger, *Pastors in Transition: Why Clergy Leave Local Church Ministry.* Eerdmans, 2005.

John W. James, Russell Friedman, and Leslie Matthews. *When Children Grieve: For Adults to Help Children Deal with Death, Divorce, Pet Loss, Moving, and Other Losses.* Harper Collins, 2001.

Marti Olsen Laney, *The Hidden Gifts of the Introverted Child: Helping Your Child Thrive in an Extroverted World*. Workman Publishing, 2012.

Fred Lehr, *Clergy Burnout: Recovering From the 70 Hour Work Week … and Other Self–Defeating Practices*. Fortress Press, 2006.

H.B. London, Jr., and Neil B. Wiseman, *Pastors at Greater Risk: Help for Pastors, Hope for the Church*. Regal Books, 2003.

H.B. London, Jr. and Neil B. Wiseman, *Your Pastor Is an Endangered Species*. Regal Books, 1996.

Susan Miller, *After the Boxes Are Unpacked*. Tyndale House Publishers, 2016.

Roy M. Oswald, *Clergy Self–Care: Finding a Balance for Effective Ministry*. Rowman & Littlefield Publishers, 1991.

Buddy Scott and R.A. "Buddy" Scott, *Relief for Hurting Parents: How to Fight for the Lives of Teenagers*. Allon Pub, 1997.

Curtis Thomas, *Practical Wisdom for Pastors: Words of Encouragement and Counsel for a Lifetime of Ministry*. Crossway, 2001.

Notes

Sources for material cited are listed here by page number.

Prologue   Heading Out

xiii   "The second motivation for writing this book stems from a survey … " The officer survey focused on causes of officer attrition. The results became a part of the author's doctoral dissertation. Of the 955 surveys distributed, 423 were completed and returned, a very favorable response rate of 44.3%. The survey results indicated that family issues play a large part in officer stress and burn–out.

Chapter 1   Well–Intentioned Failure

4   "A parent can hurt a child … " Henry Cloud and John Townsend, *Boundaries: When to Say Yes, How to Say No to Take Control of Your Life*. Zondervan, 1992.

Chapter 2   Biblical Responsibility

7   The full Mission Statement of The Salvation Army reads: "The Salvation Army, an international movement, is an evangelical part of the universal Christian church. Its

message is based on the Bible. Its ministry is motivated by the love of God. Its mission is to preach the gospel of Jesus Christ and to meet human needs in His name without discrimination."

8   "Kids are more important … " H.B. London, Jr. and Neil B. Wiseman, *Pastors at Greater Risk: Help for Pastors, Hope for the Church*. Regal Books, 2003.

Chapter 3   Pulling and Replanting Our Roots

20   "We need relationships. … " Gretchen Rubin, *Psychology Today online,* July 8, 2015.

20   "Mundane things are important to children … " The importance of details such as these to a child's feelings of security are pointed out in *When Children Grieve: For Adults to Help Children Deal with Death, Divorce, Pet Loss, Moving, and Other Losses*, by John W. James, Russell Friedman, and Leslie Matthews. HarperCollins, 2001.

22   "A study published in the Journal … " Audrey Hamilton's report, "Moving Repeatedly in Childhood Associated with Poorer Quality of Life Years Later," appeared in the June 2010 edition of *The Journal of Social and Personality Psychology*. Published by the American Psychological Association.

23   "An online publication …" Facts for Families is a series of online information sheets produced by the American Academy of Child and Adolescent Psychiatry. "Moving: Helping Children Cope" appeared in the October 2015 issue (No. 14).

Chapter 4 How Much Is Too Much?

38 Dudley Weeks, *The Eight Steps to Conflict Resolution*. Penguin Random House, 1994.

38 Susan Scott, *Fierce Conversations*. Berkley Books, 2004.

40 "Allow children to express grief ... " Cloud and Townsend, *Boundaries*.

41 Scholastic *Parents* online, "8 Warning Signs That Your Child Is Under Too Much Stress." Scholastic Inc.

43 "Sharon Brehm offered three indicators ... " These indicators were presented and discussed in an article offered online by the PACER Center: "3 Questions That Will Help You Decide If Your Child Needs Professional Help."

Chapter 5 Introvert, Extrovert, or Just Shy

51 Barbara Markway and Gregory Markway, *Painfully Shy: How to Overcome Social Anxiety and Reclaim Your Life*. St. Martin's Press, 2001.

54 Marti Olsen Laney, *The Hidden Gifts of the Introverted Child: Helping Your Child Thrive in an Extroverted World*. Workman Publishing, 2012.

Chapter 6 Preparing for the Storm

65 Thomas Curtis, *Practical Wisdom for Pastors: Words of Encouragement and Counsel for a Lifetime of Ministry*. Crossway, 2001.

67 "One of the most important things ... " Carol B. Hillman, professor of early childhood education, quoted

in Kristyn Trimble, *Moms Who Stay and Fight: How to Raise the Next Generation of Heroes*. Cedar Fort, Inc., 2018.

70   Kevin Leman, *It's Your Kid Not a Gerbil: Creating a Happier and Less–Stressed Home*. Tyndale House Publishers, 2011.

72   "Show them how important it is … " Richard Armstrong and Kirk Morledge, *Help! I'm a Pastor: A Guide to Parish Ministry*. Westminster John Knox Press, 2005.

75   London, and Wiseman, *Pastors at Greater Risk*.

76   "The pressures on pastors' children … " Armstrong and Morledge, *Help! I'm a Pastor*.

77   "Growing up is harder on kids … " Patrick Morley, *The Man in The Mirror: Solving the 24 Problems Men Face*. Zondervan, 2014.

77   "Children are like wet cement. … " Haim Ginott, *Between Parent and Child*. Harmony, 2009 First published in 1961, this book is a classic, and has helped millions of parents around the world strengthen their relationships with their children.

Chapter 7   Weathering the Storm

87   Laney, *The Hidden Gifts of the Introverted Child*.

88   "It is important to have enough respect … " Lori C. Burgan, *Moving with Kids: 25 Ways to Ease Your Family's Transition to a New Home*. Harvard Common Press, 2007.

91   James W. Pennebaker. Quoted in the online publication *The Anxiety–Free Child*, 2012.

92   Barbara Hey, "Moving Out: Soothing Your Child's Anxiety," *Blog/Parenting*, 2016.

Chapter 8   Recovery and Re–Establishment

108   Rob Lewis, *Friends*. Henry Holt and Co., 2001.

110   "A successful transition to a new school … " Burgan, *Moving with Kids*.

Chapter 9   Inside Out: A Visual Aid

122   "Depression begins with disappointment. … " Joyce Meyer, "Is It Really Possible to Beat Depression?" *The Christian Post* online newsletter, December 20, 2010.

Chapter 10   Out of Our House But
Not Out of Our Hearts

140   Jane Adams, *When Our Grown Kids Disappoint Us: Letting Go of Their Problems, Loving Them Anyway*. Free Press, 2008.

147   Allison Bottke, *Setting Boundaries with Your Adult Children: Six Steps to Hope and Healing for Struggling Parents*. Harvest House Publishers, 2008.

151   "After living with their dysfunctional behavior … " Marshall Goldsmith, *Mojo: How to Get It, How to Keep It, How to Get It Back if You Lose It*. Hachette Books, 2010.

Chapter 11   The Hazards of Ministry

155   "The perfect pastor, as far as anyone knows … " Armstrong and Morledge, *Help! I'm a Pastor*.

159   "A foundational study on this subject … " The findings of this study appear in Fred Lehr, *Clergy Burnout: Recovering from the 70 Hour Work Week … and Other Self–Defeating Practices*. Fortress Press, 2006.

160   London and Wiseman, *Pastors at Greater Risk*.

161   Barna Group Ltd., *A Profile of Protestant Pastors,* 2001.

162   H.B. London, Jr. and Neil B. Wiseman, *Your Pastor is an Endangered Species*. Regal Books, 1996.

163   Craig W. Ellison and William S. Mattila, "The Needs of Evangelical Christian Leaders in the United States," *The Journal of Psychology and Theology,* 1983.

164   "Being in the 'holy crossfire' … " Michael Morris and Priscilla Blanton, "The Influence of Work–Related Stressors on Clergy Husbands and Their Wives," *Family Relations: An Interdisciplinary Journal of Applied Family Studies,* 1994.

165   Bruce Hardy, "Pastoral Care with Clergy Children," *Review and Expositor,* 2001.

166   Lloyd Rediger, *Clergy Killers: Guidance for Pastors and Congregations under Attack*. Westminster John Knox Press, 1997.

167   Marshall Shelley, *Well–Intentioned Dragons: Ministering to Problem People in the Church*. Bethany House Publishers, 1994

169 "Skilled at meeting the needs of others ... " Susan Harrington DeVogel, "Clergy Morale: The Ups and Downs," *Christian Century,* 1986.

171 "There is considerable anxiety ... " DeVogel, "Clergy Morale: The Ups and Downs."

Chapter 12   Living in Balance

182 Richard Eyre and Linda Eyre, *Lifebalance.* Touchstone, 1997.

184 Cleveland Clinic, "What Happens to Your Body When You Don't Get Enough Sleep." *healthessentials* online magazine, 2015.

186 Hans V. Ritschard, "Family Life Style Comparison" chart, in *Doing Member Care Well: Perspectives and Practices from Around the World,* Kelly O'Donnell, ed. William Carey Library, 2002.

190 "As Christians we are called ... " Ravi Zacharias, ©RaviZacharias, Twitter, September 5, 2016.

Chapter 13   A Conclusion to the Matter

200 Donald A. Lichi, EMERGE Counseling Services. Used by permission.

www.ingramcontent.com/pod-product-compliance
Lightning Source LLC
Chambersburg PA
CBHW071525040426
42452CB00008B/892